78 top: Courtesy *The Family Handyman Magazine*, Home Service Publications, Inc., an affiliate of Reader's Digest Association, Inc. ©Copyright 1952. All rights reserved.

78 bottom: Courtesy National Gypsum Company

79 top: Courtesy Hagley Museum and Library

79 bottom left: Courtesy Florence Adams

79 bottom right: Courtesy Ventura Associates Inc. and U.S. Sales Corporation

80: Courtesy Sears, Roebuck and Company

81: Courtesy the Stanley Works. Photograph reproduced from Jeffrey L. Rodengen, *The Legend of Stanley: 150 Years of the Stanley Works*

**LOVE AFFAIR
WITH THE PAST**

83: Courtesy John Warner

84: Courtesy the Joinery Company

85: Courtesy the Boston Preservation Alliance

86 top: Courtesy *House and Garden*, copyright ©1937, by the Condé Nast Publications

86 bottom: Courtesy Mt. Vernon Ladies' Association

87 top: From *Home Builders Catalog* (Chicago: Home Builders Catalog Company, 1928)

87 bottom: Courtesy Ron Blunt Photography and the National Trust for Historic Preservation

88: Courtesy Colonial Williamsburg Foundation

90 left: ©The Sherwin-Williams Company. All rights reserved.

90 middle: Courtesy Walpole Woodworkers and Colonial Williamsburg Foundation

90 right: Courtesy *House and Garden*, copyright ©1937, by the Condé Nast Publications

91 top: Courtesy Bradbury and Bradbury Wallpapers

91 bottom: Courtesy Ornamental Mouldings Limited

92: Courtesy Aldo Rossi

93 top: Courtesy Restoration Hardware

93 bottom: Courtesy Wm. J. Rigby Company

94 all: Courtesy the Balmer Studios, Inc.

95 all: Courtesy WGBH Television

SELECTED BIBLIOGRAPHY

This bibliography includes a select list of secondary works that informed the historical interpretation contained within this book as well as some of the more important primary documents on which its argument rests:

Albrecht, Donald, ed. *World War II and the American Dream: How Wartime Building Changed a Nation.* Washington, D.C.: National Building Museum; Cambridge, MA: MIT Press, 1995.

Better Homes and Gardens Handyman's Book.
Des Moines: Meredith Publishing Company, 1951.

Blum, John Morton. *V Was for Victory: Politics and American Culture During World War II.* New York: Harcourt Brace Jovanovich, 1976.

Brand, Stewart. *How Buildings Learn: What Happens After They're Built.* New York: Viking, 1994.

"The Building of America." Special issue of *Do-It-Yourself Retailing* (June 1986).

Clark, Clifford Edward, Jr. *The American Family Home, 1800–1960.* Chapel Hill: University of North Carolina Press, 1986.

Corn, Joseph J. "Educating the Enthusiast: Print and the Popularization of Technical Knowledge." In *Possible Dreams: Enthusiasm for Technology in America,* edited by John L. Wright. Dearborn, MI: Henry Ford Museum & Greenfield Village, 1992.

————. "'Textualizing Technics': Owners' Manuals and the Reading of Objects." In *Material Culture: The Shape of the Field,* edited by Ann Smart Martin and J. Ritchie Garrison. Wilmington, DE: Winterthur Museum and Library, forthcoming.

Cowan, Ruth Schwartz. *More Work for Mother: The Ironies of Household Technology from the Open Hearth to the Microwave.* New York: Basic Books, 1983.

Foy, Jessica H. and Karal Ann **Marling,** eds. *The Arts and the American Home, 1890–1930.* Knoxville, TN: University of Tennessee Press, 1994.

Foy, Jessica H. and Thomas J. **Schelereth,** eds. *American Home Life, 1880–1930: A Social History of Spaces and Services.* Knoxville, TN: University of Tennessee Press, 1992.

Friedan, Betty. *The Feminine Mystique.* New York: W. W. Norton, 1963.

Gelber, Steven M. "Do-It-Yourself: Constructing, Repairing and Maintaining Domestic Masculinity." *American Quarterly* 49 (March 1997): 66–112.

————. "A Job You Can't Lose: Work and Hobbies in the Great Depression." *Journal of Social History* 24, no. 4 (June 1991): 741–66.

Gilbert, James B. *Another Chance: Postwar America, 1945–1985.* Belmont, CA: Wadsworth Publishing, Inc., 1986.

Gottfried, Herbert. "Building the Picture: Trading on the Imagery of Production and Design." *Winterthur Portfolio* 27, no. 4 (Winter 1992): 235–53.

Grier, Katherine C. *Culture and Comfort: Parlor-Making and Middle-Class Identity, 1850–1930.* Washington, D.C.: Smithsonian Institution Press, 1997.

Halttunen, Karen. "From Parlor to Living Room: Domestic Space, Interior Decoration, and the Culture of Personality." In *Consuming Visions: Accumulation and Display of Goods in America, 1880–1920,* edited by Simon Bronner. New York: W. W. Norton, 1979.

Hine, Thomas. *The Total Package: The Evolution and Secret Meanings of Boxes, Bottles, Cans and Tubes.* Boston: Little, Brown, 1995.

Hodgins, Eric. *Mr. Blandings Builds His Dream House.* New York: Simon and Schuster, 1946.

Horrigan, Brian. "The Home of Tomorrow, 1927–1945." In *Imagining Tomorrow,* edited by Joseph J. Corn. Cambridge, MA: MIT Press, 1986.

Hoy, Suellen. *Chasing Dirt: The American Pursuit of Cleanliness.* New York: Oxford University Press, 1995.

Huff, Darrell. "We've Found a Substitute for Income." *Harper's Magazine* (October 1953): 26–33.

Jackson, Kenneth T. *Crabgrass Frontier: The Suburbanization of the United States.* New York: Oxford University Press, 1985.

Jarreau, Philippe. *Du Bricolage: Archeologie de la Maison.* Paris: Centre Georges Pompidou, Centre de Creation Industrielle, 1985.

Jenkins, Virginia Scott. *The Lawn: A History of an American Obsession.* Washington, D.C. and London: Smithsonian Institution Press, 1994.

Jennings, Jan. "Controlling Passion: The Turn-of-the-Century Wallpaper Dilemma." *Winterthur Portfolio* 31, no. 4 (Winter 1996): 243–64.

————. "Drawing on the Vernacular Interior." *Winterthur Portfolio* 27, no. 4 (Winter 1992): 255–79.

Jester, Thomas C., ed. *Twentieth-Century Building Materials: History and Conservation.* New York: McGraw-Hill, 1995.

Keats, John. *The Crack in the Picture Window.* Boston: Houghton Mifflin, 1956.

Kelly, Barbara M. *Expanding the American Dream: Building and Rebuilding Levittown.* Albany: State University of New York Press, 1993.

Kidder, Tracy. *House.* Boston: Houghton Mifflin, 1985.

Lifshey, Earl. *The Housewares Story: A History of the American Housewares Industry.* Chicago: National Housewares Manufacturers Association, 1973.

Lupton, Ellen. *Mechanical Brides: Women and Machines in the Home and Office.* New York: Cooper-Hewitt National Museum of Design, Smithsonian Institution, and Princeton Architectural Press, 1993.

Lupton, Ellen, and J. Abbott **Miller.** *The Bathroom, the Kitchen, and the Aesthetics of Waste: A Process of Elimination.* New York: Kiosk/Princeton Architectural Press, 1992.

Mack, Arien, ed. *Home: A Place in the World.* New York: New York University Press, 1993.

Macleod, David. *Building Character in the American Boy: The Boy Scouts, YMCA, and Their Forerunners, 1870–1920.* Madison: University of Wisconsin Press, 1983.

Marling, Karal Ann. *As Seen on TV: The Visual Culture of Everyday Life in the 1950s.* Cambridge, MA: Harvard University Press, 1994.

Marsh, Margaret. *Suburban Lives.* New Brunswick, NJ: Rutgers University Press, 1990.

May, Elaine Tyler. *Homeward Bound: American Families in the Cold War Era.* New York: Basic Books, 1988.

Moss, Roger W., ed. *Paint in America: The Color of Historic Buildings.* Washington, D.C.: Preservation Press, National Trust for Historic Preservation, 1994.

"The New Do-It-Yourself Market." *Business Week* (14 June 1952): 60–62, 64, 66, 69–70, 72, 74, 76.

"Power Tools: The Newest Home Appliance." *Industrial Design* (February 1954): 30–37.

Pursell, Carroll. "Toys, Technology and Sex Roles in America, 1920–1940." In *Dynamos and Virgins Revisited: Women and Technological Change in History, An Anthology*, edited by Martha Moore Trescott. Metuchen, NJ: The Scarecrow Press, 1979.

Reader's Digest Complete Do-It-Yourself Manual. Pleasantville, NY: Reader's Digest Association, Inc., 1973.

Rodengen, Jeffrey L. *The Legend of Stanley: 150 Years of the Stanley Works.* Fort Lauderdale, FL: Write Stuff Syndicate, Inc., 1996.

Roland, Albert. "Do-It-Yourself: A Walden for the Millions?" *American Quarterly* 10 (Summer 1958): 154–64.

Rybczynski, Witold. *Home: A Short History of an Idea.* New York: Viking, 1986.

———. *The Most Beautiful House in the World.* New York: Viking, 1989.

Shi, David. *The Simple Life: Plain Living and High Thinking in American Culture.* New York: Oxford University Press, 1985.

"The Shoulder Trade." *Time* (2 August 1954): 62–68.

Simpson, Pamela H. *Cheap, Quick and Easy: Imitative Architectural Materials, 1870–1930.* Knoxville, TN: University of Tennessee Press, forthcoming.

Staten, Vince. *Did Monkeys Invent the Monkey Wrench? Hardware Stores and Hardware Stories.* New York: Simon and Schuster, 1996.

Stilgoe, John R. *Borderland: Origins of the American Suburb, 1820–1939.* New Haven: Yale University Press, 1988.

———. *Common Landscape of America, 1580 to 1845.* New Haven: Yale University Press, 1982.

Strasser, Susan. *Never Done: A History of American Housework.* New York: Pantheon, 1982.

———. *Satisfaction Guaranteed: The Making of the American Mass Market.* New York: Pantheon, 1989.

Tobey, Ronald C. *Technology as Freedom: The New Deal and the Electrical Modernization of the American Home.* Berkeley: University of California Press, 1996.

The War-Time Guide Book. New York: Popular Science Publishing Company, Inc., 1942.

Weiss, Marc. *The Rise of the Community Builders: The Real Estate Industry and Urban Land Planning.* New York: Columbia University Press, 1987.

Whitman, Roger C. *First Aid for the Ailing House: A Complete Basic Manual for the Care, Repair, and Maintenance of the Home.* New York: Pocket Books, Inc., 1958.

Wright, Gwendolyn. *Building the Dream: A Social History of Housing in America.* Cambridge, MA: MIT Press, 1981.

———. *Moralism and the Model Home: Domestic Architecture and Cultural Conflict, 1873–1913.* Chicago: University of Chicago Press, 1980.

Wright, John L., ed. *Possible Dreams: Enthusiasm for Technology in America.* Dearborn, MI: Henry Ford Museum & Greenfield Village, 1992.

A number of periodicals were especially useful in researching *Do It Yourself.* Magazines such as *American Home, Better Homes and Gardens, House Beautiful, House and Garden,* and *Sunset* all devoted increasing attention to home improvement throughout the century. *McCall's* and *American Magazine* also included many articles about do-it-yourself in the 1950s. *The Family Handyman, Popular Mechanics,* and *Popular Science* were among the specialized magazines aimed primarily at male do-it-yourselfers. The trade publications *Sales Management* and *Modern Packaging* contained evidence of changing trends in the sales and marketing of home-improvement products.

Acknowledgments

DO IT YOURSELF is the result of the hard work and dedication of an exceptional team. Curatorial Assistant Michael R. Harrison contributed thoughtful analysis and sharp wit to selecting images, reading drafts, and writing captions. Jennifer Bride helped to secure photographic reproductions and copyright permissions. Karen Eisenberg edited a draft of the manuscript and made useful comments at an early stage. Karen Moon conducted most of the research for chapter five and contributed to many other portions of the book. My thanks go as well to the interns who helped with research: Samuel Isenstadt, Lara Day Kozak, Patricia Reixach, Abraham Sheppard, and Victoria Young. In addition, Susan Henshaw Jones, Mary Konsoulis, and Joseph Rosa provided support along the way. The book's visual appearance and overall quality owe much to our collaboration with J. Abbott Miller, Paul Carlos, and Ji Byol Lee at Design/Writing/Research, and with Kevin Lippert and Sara Stemen at Princeton Architectural Press.

I AM ALSO GRATEFUL to my colleagues outside the Museum. Steven Lubar and Susan Smulyan served as historical consultants, offering constructive feedback and advice at every stage. At the Smithsonian Institution's National Museum of American History, Peter Liebhold, David Shayt, Rodris Roth, and Bill Yeingst provided enthusiastic encouragement and assistance. Donald Albrecht, Jane Becker, Dan Bluestone, Ed Chappell, Richard Cheek, Joe Corn, Kathy Franz, Harvey Green, David Hounshell, Janet Hutchison, Tom Jester, Todd Langston, Shelley Nickles, Peggy Shaffer, Pam Simpson, Bruce Sinclair, Kathy Steen, Susan Strasser, Selma Thomas, Elizabeth White, and Susan Williams all participated in brainstorming sessions and made helpful suggestions. At the television program *This Old House*, Russ Morash, Bruce Irving, and Kim Cotter answered questions about contemporary issues in restoration and renovation. Numerous museums, companies, and collectors loaned images. Finally, I would like to thank my husband, Jon Haber, for his engaging companionship throughout the process.

ABOUT THE AUTHOR

Carolyn M. Goldstein is a curator in the exhibitions department at the National Building Museum. She holds a Ph.D. in history from the University of Delaware. Her next book will explore the relationship between the home-economics movement and consumer culture in 20th-century America.

Notes

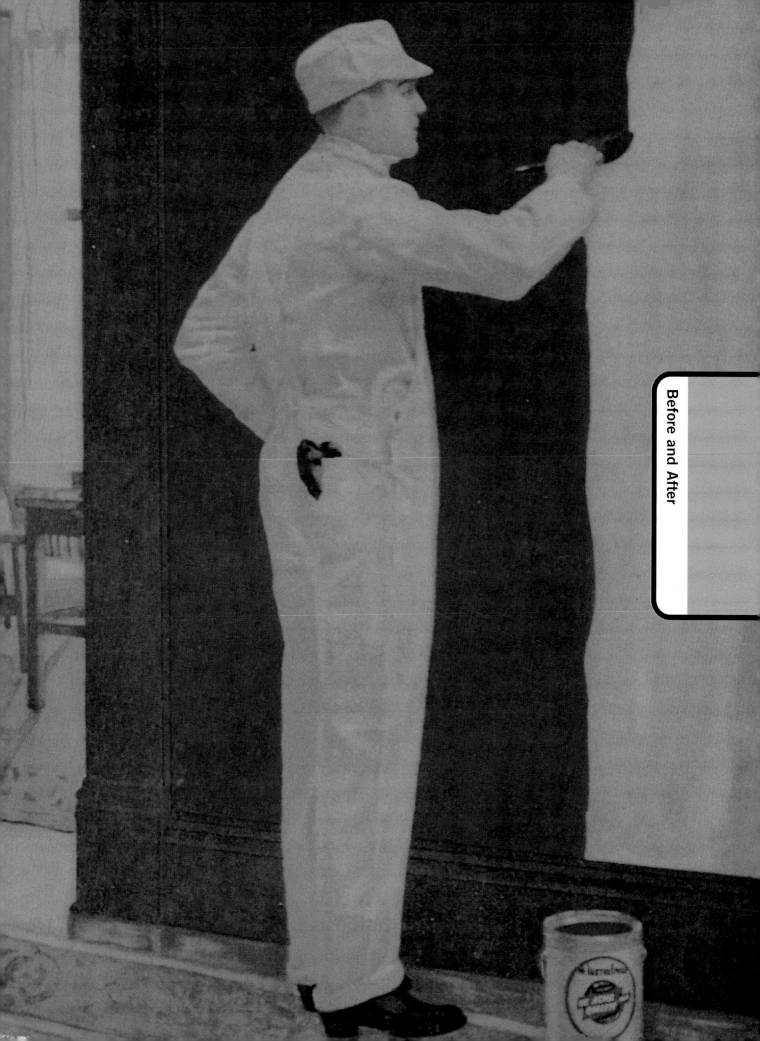

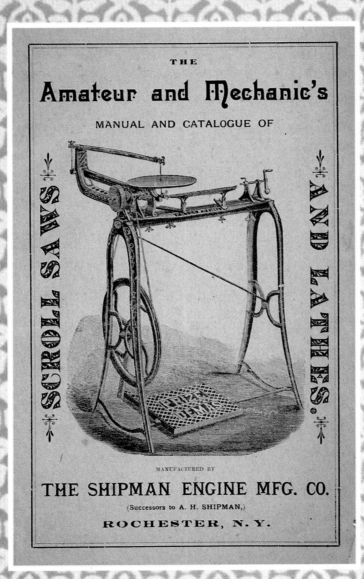

THE

Amateur and Mechanic's

MANUAL AND CATALOGUE OF

SCROLL SAWS

AND LATHES

MANUFACTURED BY

THE SHIPMAN ENGINE MFG. CO.

(Successors to A. H. SHIPMAN,)

ROCHESTER, N.Y.

TOP Cover of *The Amateur and Mechanic's Manual and Catalogue of Scroll Saws and Lathes*, 1887

PREVIOUS PAGE A professional painter, from the *Acme Quality Painting Guide Book*, ca. 1910

Before and After

The origins of the do-it-yourself idea can be
traced to around 1900, when home improvement began to assume
a self-conscious character and to play an active role in American
culture. Middle-class Americans began to show a greater interest in
the manual arts, handicrafts, and home workshops. Mass-circulation
magazines began providing their readers with an expanding body
of information about home remodeling and repair. By disseminating
a visual language of "before" and "after," these publications helped
make home remodeling a central feature of American domestic life
and consumer culture. Manufacturers of building materials, appliances, and home fittings gradually reached outside the construction
trades and marketed their products to consumers by suggesting
new possibilities for transforming one's home. Government loan-
guaranty programs initiated during the 1930s placed homeownership
within the reach of growing numbers of families and encouraged
them to modernize their dwellings. Between 1900 and 1940, all of
these factors combined to create a home-improvement infrastructure
that changed the way Americans viewed their homes, sowing the
seeds of the do-it-yourself idea.

The Home Workshop

TO EXECUTE MOST REPAIR and remodeling projects—and to achieve modernization as defined by magazines, manufacturers, and government officials—early-20th-century homeowners relied on the skills and expertise of professional craftsmen and contractors. Structural changes or additions to the home required carpenters, masons, roofers, and glaziers. Decorative work called for the special abilities of painters, wallpaper hangers, plasterers, and tile layers. In addition to having the skills to execute remodeling projects, these craftsmen were familiar with the requisite materials and tools and knew where and how to purchase them. Many middle-class homeowners were more interested in the professional quality of the results than in the technical process itself. Few American homeowners assumed that they could make improvements on their own.

STARTING IN THE LATE 19TH CENTURY, however, middle-class Americans became interested in learning manual skills as a hobby and, eventually, in applying them to home improvement. White-collar office workers and other professionals had more leisure time than in the past. In addition, living in a modern industrial society led many to romanticize craftsmanship and handcrafted appearances.

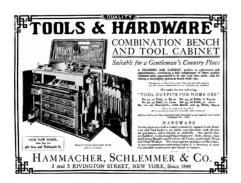

Combination bench and tool cabinet, from a Hammacher, Schlemmer & Co. advertisement, 1903

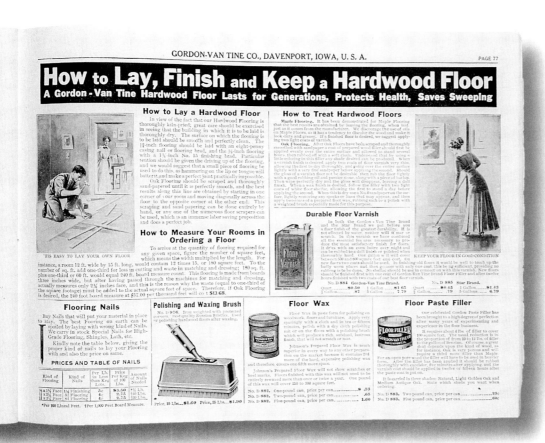

Homeowner laying a hardwood floor while his wife looks on, from a Gordon-Van Tine Co. advertisement, ca. 1910

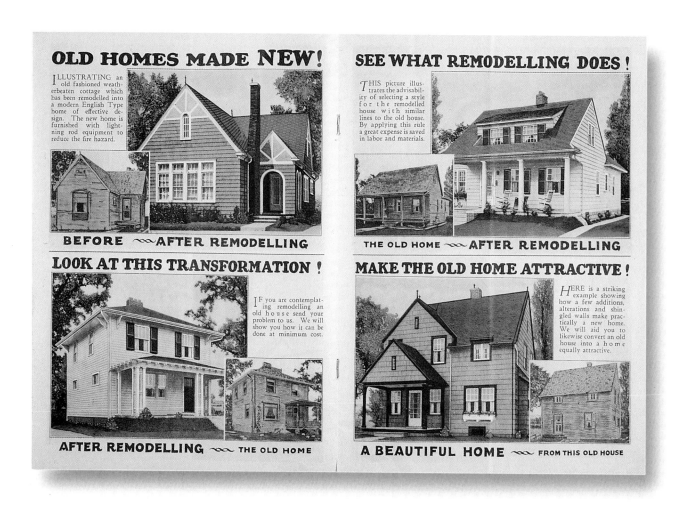

OLD HOMES MADE NEW!

ILLUSTRATING an old fashioned weatherbeaten cottage which has been remodelled into a modern English Type home of effective design. The new home is furnished with lightning rod equipment to reduce the fire hazard.

BEFORE ∿ AFTER REMODELLING

SEE WHAT REMODELLING DOES!

THIS picture illustrates the advisability of selecting a style for the remodelled house with similar lines to the old house. By applying this rule a great expense is saved in labor and materials.

THE OLD HOME ∿ AFTER REMODELLING

LOOK AT THIS TRANSFORMATION!

IF you are contemplating remodelling an old house send your problem to us. We will show you how it can be done at minimum cost.

AFTER REMODELLING ∿ THE OLD HOME

MAKE THE OLD HOME ATTRACTIVE!

HERE is a striking example showing how a few additions, alterations and shingled walls make practically a new home. We will aid you to likewise convert an old house into a home equally attractive.

A BEAUTIFUL HOME ∿ FROM THIS OLD HOUSE

TOP Like many manufacturers, Liberty Lumber & Coal Co. advertised its products by demonstrating the aesthetic benefits of remodeling, 1927

OPPOSITE PAGE Cover of the *House and Garden Modernization Portfolio*, September 1938

upper-middle-class audience to hire architects to design remodeling solutions. By the end of the decade, most home magazines had established similar competitions.10

THROUGH REMODELING CONTESTS AND ARTICLES that contained comparative "before" and "after" photographs and specific instructions, magazines advised, taught, and inspired readers to make their homes conform to modern standards of design. "Modernization" became the order of the day: editors advocated the removal of late-19th-century Victorian exterior features such as porches, dormers, and towers, and also encouraged homeowners to simplify and open up interior spaces by dismantling walls, doors, and other partitions. A living room and a dining room could, for example, be combined to make "one large bright room."11 Ideal modern homes were stylistically unified, efficient in their use of space, and easy to clean. They featured new technologies and products such as oil-fired furnaces, electrical kitchen appliances, and porcelain bathroom fixtures and tiles which extended the modernization ideal into all corners of the house.

cottage plans and inspirational "before" and "after" views that readers planning to build new homes could take to builders to be copied.[9]

THE PROLIFERATION OF HOME-IMPROVEMENT MAGAZINES and their increased circulation to a mass audience around 1900 reinforced popular interest in the home and its improvement. New publications such as *House and Garden* (1901) and *House Beautiful* (1896) often included articles about room decorating and furnishing. By the 1920s, these magazines also regularly offered articles about interior and exterior remodeling. With at least a dozen home-related magazines on the newsstands every month, people could read about remodeling in greater detail than ever before. This exposure to new ideas about architecture, interior decoration, and domestic living led many Americans to want to update their own homes.

ATTENTION TO HOME improvement in these magazines culminated with the sponsorship of remodeling competitions. *Better Homes and Gardens* inaugurated the trend with its 1932 "How We Rebuilt" contest. The editors invited readers to submit "before" and "after" photographs of their renovation projects with a short letter describing the changes. They offered eight prizes ranging from $5 to $100 for remodeling projects—"no matter how great or small"—that enhanced the comfort, convenience, or aesthetic appearance of a home. The contest became a popular annual event, drawing 150,000 entrants in its first five years. A similar competition at *House Beautiful* offered larger cash prizes to inspire the magazine's

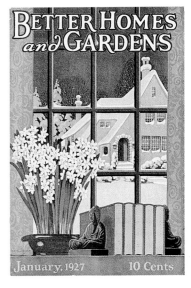

Cover of *Better Homes and Gardens*, January 1927

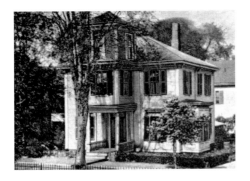
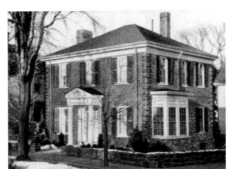
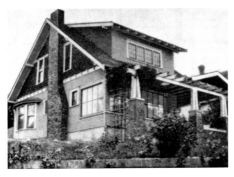
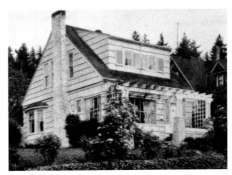

Before and after views of two renovation-contest-winning houses, from *Better Homes and Gardens*, August 1934

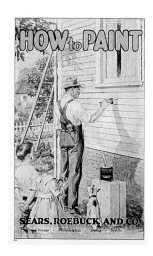

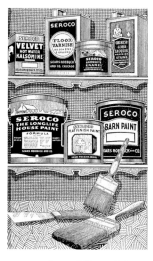

FAR TOP Cover of *How to Paint*, Sears, Roebuck and Company's painting guide, ca. 1920

TOP Sears painting products, from *How to Paint*, ca. 1920

The house which adequately fulfilled all the needs of the family twenty years ago is now found to be inconvenient, wastefully planned and shabby.
HOUSE AND GARDEN MODERNIZATION PORTFOLIO, 1938[8]

and steel siding as well as paints and varnishes for both indoor and outdoor projects. By selling the necessary tools and supplies, Sears also made it easy for nonspecialists to take on repair projects. Although Sears's early catalogs listed tools in separate sections aimed at specialized trades, its later editions regrouped these products to address the needs of amateur builders. As early as 1901, Sears listed kits of tools packaged for "saving time and carpenters and wagon-makers bills." The 1905 catalog advertised the Acme Beauty Mantel, which "[did] not require the services of a brick mason" for installation. Kits of all kinds—for painting, odd jobs, and repairs—became increasingly common features of Sears's growing list of items that individual homeowners could use to repair or improve their dwellings. In addition to offering entire houses for sale, the company's millwork section sold sashes, doors, and moldings. By 1930, within five years of opening its first retail stores, Sears had created a Building Material catalog offering "everything you need to build, remodel, modernize, or repair your house," as well as a Builders' Service department to support it.[6]

IN ADDITION TO PRODUCTS, Sears also provided its customers with an array of services and advice on how to repair and remodel their homes. Its catalogs often contained instructions for using the featured building products. Separate publications introduced novices to specific tasks. For example, *How to Paint*, a booklet first published around 1905, claimed: "anyone, without any previous experience, can do any job of painting successfully." Wallpaper sample books included free instructions on how to hang wallpaper. By 1920 Sears had established a paper-trimming service that would precut wallpaper to specified sizes. Finally, by providing cost estimates for specific projects, ideas for saving money, and credit payment plans, Sears helped make home improvement affordable for more and more Americans.[7]

Magazines and Modernization

IN THE 19TH CENTURY, the home had become defined as a refuge from the workaday world of industry. For a new middle class, domesticity had become identified with issues of status and identity. A growing body of prescriptive literature about the home celebrated "the cult of domesticity" among middle-class women. Books like Catherine Beecher's *Treatise on Domestic Economy* (1848) and magazines such as *Godey's Lady's Book* gave advice about home decorating, providing tips on such subjects as color schemes, house plants, and furniture placement. Such publications offered house and

Beginning around 1900, American proponents of the arts and crafts movement promoted an interest in "simple" styles of furniture and domestic architecture. Magazines like *The Craftsman* celebrated artisanal craft and provided readers with instructions about how to construct simple built-in bookcases, desks, and dining nooks.[2] The modern, less elaborate designs of the movement were relatively easy for an amateur to make.

NEW PUBLICATIONS RESPONDED to this interest in handicrafts and provided advice and instructions to a growing amateur audience. In the 1910s and 1920s, *Popular Science* and *Popular Mechanics* — first published in 1872 and 1902 respectively — began to include articles to guide novices through small craft and construction projects as well as basic household repairs. Eventually these magazines began to encourage homeowners to undertake some of their own remodeling. According to historian Steven Gelber, the phrase "do-it-yourself" made an early appearance in a 1912 article encouraging homeowners to do their own interior painting rather than to hire professional painters.[3] Success with how-to sections providing illustrated directions for home-repair and -improvement projects led magazine publishers to compile books like *Tinkering with Tools* (1925), *Things to Make in Your Home Workshop* (1930), and *Fix It Yourself* (1929).[4] Addressing a new middle-class audience for whom the home was becoming a hobby, these publications encouraged home repair and maintenance in part because it saved money, but primarily because it was pleasurable.

UNEMPLOYMENT AND UNDEREMPLOYMENT caused by the Great Depression furthered the growing interest in "hobbies." Hobbies allowed Americans to participate in the work ethic, use free time productively, and learn job skills, even if they were unemployed.[5] As handicraft hobbyists became more numerous, they carved out places in their homes to make model trains and airplanes, furniture, and other freestanding wooden items. In basements, garages, and other spaces converted into home workshops, home craftsmen gained the skills and confidence to execute functional projects around the house. Many amateur craftsmen took on increasingly ambitious home-improvement projects. After applying woodworking know-how to basic repairs, they went on to small-scale renovations, including constructing built-in shelving and storage space. The growing popularity of home workshops helped establish an atmosphere in which fixing up an unfinished room on one's own seemed possible.

MAIL-ORDER CATALOG COMPANIES supported this trend by making the appropriate tools and equipment available to a mass market. Sears, Roebuck and Company, for example, initially aimed its catalog at rural families who regularly upgraded their house exteriors as part of farm operation and maintenance. It supplied metal roofing

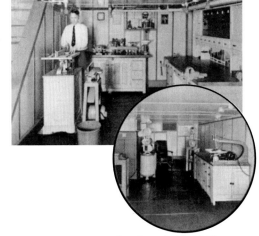

Two views of Philadelphian John A. Mahon's basement workshop, built in the 1930s, as featured in Delta Manufacturing Company's woodworking magazine *The Deltagram*, October 1941

HOUSE & GAR

Modernization Portfolio

Section II

Before

After

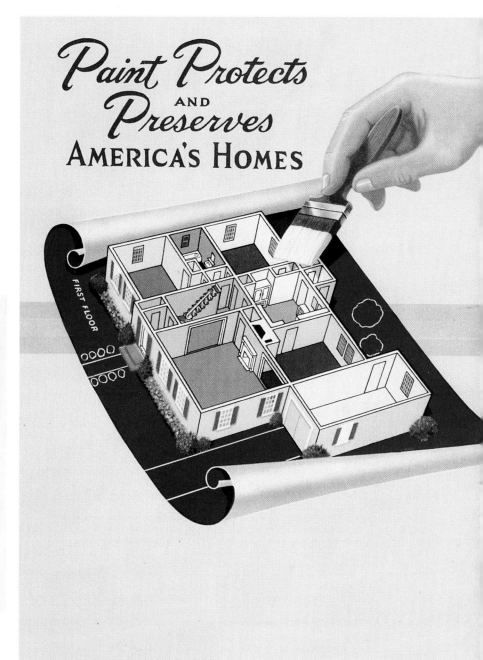

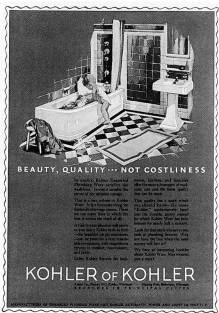

CLOCKWISE FROM TOP

The modern bathroom according to
the Kohler Company, 1925

Back-cover illustration from
Color Style Ideas, a Benjamin
Moore paint advice book, 1942

Advertisement for Armstrong
linoleum, 1924

Advertisement for Sealex linoleum
floor covering, 1929

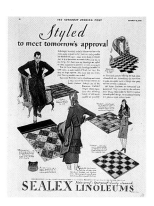

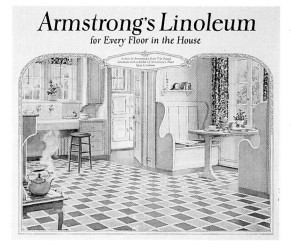

Material Possibilities

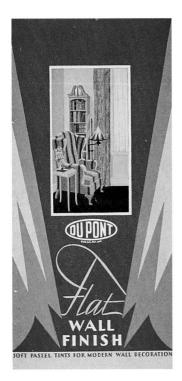

Du Pont flat wall finish brochure,
ca. 1930

THE DEVELOPMENT AND DISTRIBUTION of new building materials and fixtures in the first three decades of the century altered house-construction techniques as well as remodeling methods and styles. After World War I, a growing number of manufacturers began advertising directly to consumers through the popular magazines. By emphasizing the modern effects that could be achieved with their floor coverings, decorative finishes, and new appliances, these companies presented middle-class consumers with a wide range of possibilities for home improvement and modernization.

BY THE 1920S AND 1930S, consumers could choose from a growing array of machine-made materials for improving their homes. Asphalt and asbestos shingles, as well as simulated masonry products such as Permastone, could be applied directly over original wood or brick exterior walls to give the home a new appearance. For interior refinishing, a variety of wallboards simplified the process and lowered the cost of erecting new walls. Gypsum wallboard—a pressed-plaster compound also known as drywall—was marketed under the brand name Sheetrock by the United States Gypsum Company. This ready-made product eliminated the traditional steps used by carpenters and plasterers to create smooth wall surfaces.[12] U.S. Gypsum and its competitors promoted gypsum wallboard as the solution to homeowers' remodeling needs. Sales of the material began to take off in the 1920s as consumers discovered that it enabled them quickly and easily to convert attics and basements into livable space and to adjust the placement of interior walls as called for by modernization advocates. Plaster and gypsum companies also produced precut metal arches that facilitated the creation of wide openings between rooms. The arches simplified plastering work and allowed homeowners to replace dark, rectilinear woodwork with light, clean, and smooth curvilinear edges that conformed to modern aesthetic standards.

BATHROOMS AND KITCHENS became the standard-bearers of modernization in many homes. The availability of newly mass-produced porcelain and ceramic fixtures—toilets, bathtubs, and floor and wall tiles—encouraged homeowners to transform their bathrooms into idealized havens of sanitation and cleanliness. Manufacturers of gas and electric appliances presented kitchens as models of efficient work space, promoting streamlined stoves and refrigerators, as well as built-in cabinets and continuous-height work surfaces that provided ease of movement and a unified appearance.[13] By updating kitchens and bathrooms in these ways, families with limited resources could obtain improved hygiene, new technologies in the home, and a

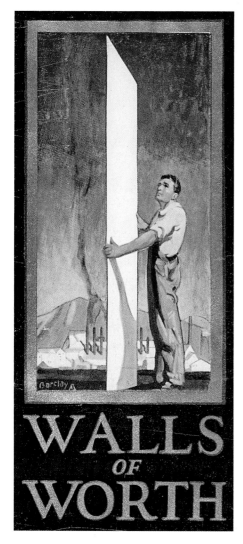

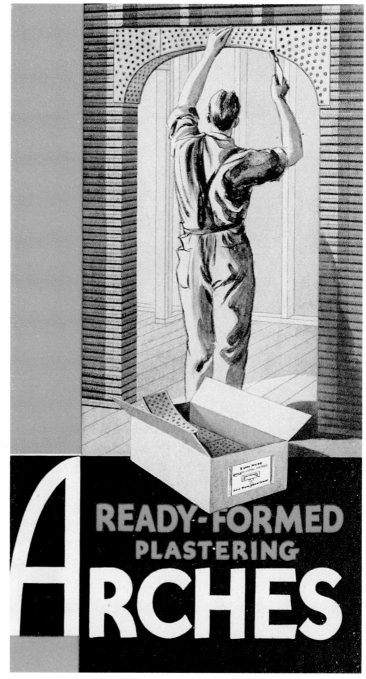

modern aesthetic. People with limited funds for modernization
typically spent them on these spaces.

FOR THOSE HOMEOWNERS who lacked the means to remodel an entire
bathroom or kitchen, floor coverings offered more affordable modernization possibilities. Linoleum, a composite material of linseed oil,
ground cork dust, gums, and pigments pressed onto a canvas backing,
was developed in England in the 1860s as an alternative to floor
oilcloth, a heavy, painted canvas. By 1900 there were a handful

of linoleum producers in the United States, the largest of which was the Armstrong Cork and Tile Company. Armstrong aggressively marketed the floor covering as a remodeling material. Beginning in the late 1910s, the company advertised linoleum in a number of women's magazines as well as the *Saturday Evening Post*. The advertisements promoted the material's use in replacing cracked floors and in "home beautification." Many ads also trumpeted linoleum's "modern" qualities: its cleanliness, durability, and resiliency. These qualities accounted for the machine-made floor covering's predominant use in kitchens, bathrooms, and entrance halls. By 1918 Armstrong listed 380 designs in its linoleum pattern book, including mosaic and imitation carpet patterns. Relatively cheap and easy to install, linoleum was popular throughout the 1920s and 1930s, although its sales were eventually surpassed by felt-base floor covering, a less expensive alternative.[14]

AS NEW MACHINE-MADE MATERIALS like linoleum entered the market, producers of hardware and building supplies stepped up their efforts to convince homeowners of their products' renovation possibilities. For example, paint manufacturers, who had traditionally aimed their marketing at professional painters, now worked to establish direct communication with consumers. They issued pamphlets and "color guides" to help homeowners buy better paint jobs, select professional painters, and discover paint's decorative possibilities. Sherwin-Williams, for example, distributed 2,500,000 advice pamphlets in 1935.[15] Many paint companies hired interior designers to assist painters and their customers with decorating decisions. At the Benjamin Moore Company in New York City, "Betty Moore" headed an advisory service devoted to marketing paint to homeowners.

BY THE LATE 1920S, building-supply and hardware manufacturers had self-consciously turned to the home-renovation market as source of profit. By forming the Home Modernizing Bureau in 1928, representatives from the building and hardware industries joined forces to promote the use of their products in home renovation. The bureau opened offices throughout the United States and launched advertising campaigns in local newspapers. These campaigns aimed to trigger a "modernization movement" that would remodel approximately three out of every five American residences, or some twelve million homes—a potential market of $24 billion! Design experts, chosen by the Home Modernizing Bureau and set up in offices around the country, promoted modern standards of beauty, comfort, and convenience—especially if they could be realized through new commercial products.[16]

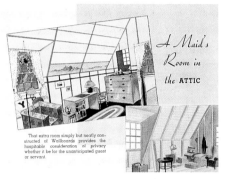

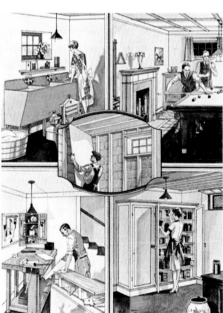

FAR TOP A maid's room created with Bird Wallboards, 1935

TOP The finishing of basements became popular after the introduction of gas- and oil-fired furnaces in the 1920s and 1930s, leading wallboard manufacturers to suggest uses for such renovated spaces, as in this Gold Bond advertisement, 1930.

The National Housing Act and the Better Housing Program

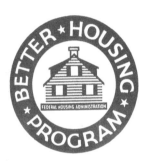

This emblem appeared on Federal Housing Administration publications as well as in advertising for materials and services that could be purchased with government-insured home-improvement loans, 1934.

THE NUMBER OF PRIVATELY OWNED HOMES more than tripled between 1890 and 1930.[17] Homeownership took off even more after 1934 when the United States government began guaranteeing home-mortgage loans, and the popularity of home improvement increased along with it.

THE PASSAGE OF THE NATIONAL HOUSING ACT OF 1934 created the Federal Housing Administration (FHA) and a system of federally guarantied bank mortgages. Before the FHA, only the wealthiest Americans could afford to own homes, but the new FHA guarantied loans with a down payment of only ten percent and made the dream of homeownership accessible to unprecedented numbers of families.

IN ADDITION TO GUARANTYING LOANS for home purchases, the National Housing Act provided federally guarantied loans of up to $2,000 for "repairs, alterations, or improvements" to existing single-family dwellings. The administration's Better Housing Program, which promoted these repair-loan guaranties, was designed to achieve two goals: to stimulate the construction industry in a depressed economy, and to improve housing conditions. The program significantly furthered the latter by providing a way for many homeowners to make basic repairs to their dwellings. The FHA's first home-improvement loan was for $125 to John P. Powers of Cloquet, Minnesota, for painting his house, repairing his roof, and installing a water tank.[19] A 1939 survey estimated that homeowners typically borrowed approximately $400, and used the loans most often to repaint their homes' exteriors, install new heating systems, and electrify their kitchens.[20] In its first three years, the FHA issued nearly 1.5 million home-modernization loans out of approximately eleven million owner-occupied homes. In other words, one in eight American homeowners had an FHA Title I loan between 1934 and 1937, making the Better Housing Program quite visible in the public eye.[21]

TO ENCOURAGE MORE AMERICANS to take advantage of the Better Housing Program, the FHA mounted an ambitious publicity campaign. In one of a series of newsreel-style films, modern architect William Lescaze showed how he had remodeled his "shabby brownstone house" in New York City into a fully modern living space. Another film, entitled "Attic Magic," showed how "a few workmen and a modernization loan" could transform "useless space" into a bedroom, a study, or a children's playroom. More than twenty-seven million viewers saw these promotions in the first year, according to one estimate.[22] The agency's radio programs brought the voice of Uncle Sam

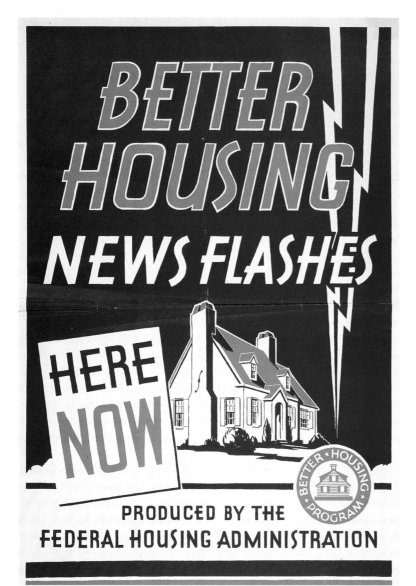

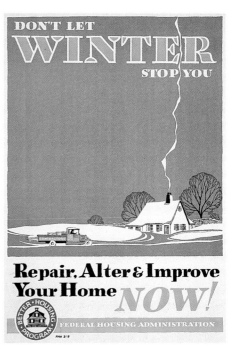

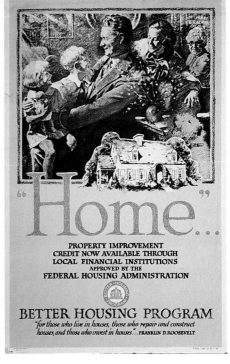

FHA posters, mid-1930s

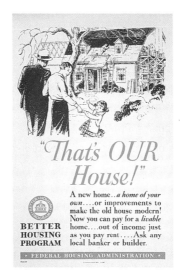

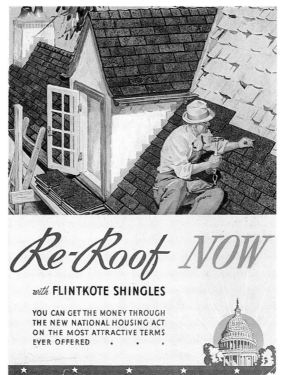

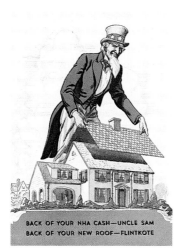

BACK OF YOUR NHA CASH—UNCLE SAM
BACK OF YOUR NEW ROOF—FLINTKOTE

TOP Flintkote advertised that under the National Housing Act, Uncle Sam would make home-renewal projects possible, 1935.

TOP RIGHT Flintkote urged home-owners to replace their roofs, 1935.

into American homes and used dramatic presentations to describe how to obtain FHA loans for remodeling projects.[23] FHA posters also celebrated the Better Homes Program by defining home repair and remodeling as patriotic activities.

THE BUILDING AND BUILDING-PRODUCTS INDUSTRIES helped spread the word about the new federally guaranteed financing mechanisms and offered monthly payment plans of their own. The loan system, after all, encouraged homeowners to use commercial products, whether paint, shingles, or bathroom fixtures. For the same reasons, magazines such as *Better Homes and Gardens*—which had campaigned for a comprehensive national home-building and home-improvement plan in the early 1930s—publicized these programs and instructed readers how to take advantage of them.

BY 1940 HOME IMPROVEMENT was well on its way to becoming a self-conscious part of American culture and identity. Middle-class consumers had an increasingly wide array of resources and materials at their fingertips as they contemplated new ways of transforming their houses into homes.

Ingenuity at Home and Abroad

The men who went out unable to drive a nail, and who learned in the interim to make a camp telephone out of the wiring of a wrecked Messerschmidt, using the headsets of a hastily abandoned Gestapo office and a jeep brakedrum as a bell—their return should mean a new era in homemade living improvements.
CAPTAIN ALFRED FRIENDLY, *HOUSE BEAUTIFUL*, JANUARY 1945[2]

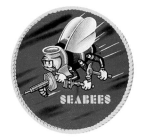

TOP The insignia of the Seabees, the U.S. Navy's construction battalions

BOTTOM Cartoon drawn by Bill Mauldin in Italy, 1944

BOTTOM RIGHT Barrett shingles advertising card from World War II, suggesting home repair and improvement as patriotic obligations

THE EXPERIENCE OF WORLD WAR II and the propaganda surrounding it led Americans to hope for and expect a better life in peacetime. Dreams of improved housing, a fulfilling family life, and a cornucopia of consumer goods helped men and women to endure the war's shortages and uncertainties. At the same time, wartime experiences both at home and overseas predisposed Americans to undertake renovations on their own by providing them with the skills and confidence needed to make their domestic aspirations a reality.

BETWEEN 1940 AND 1945, $23 million was spent on defense-related construction, as the demands of war led manufacturers to construct entire company towns to house workers close to vital centers of weapons and munitions production. Similarly, the United States government funded a building program of unprecedented scale to erect training facilities and military bases at home and abroad. Both industrial and military construction drew vast numbers of men and women into the war effort. At expanded shipyards and aircraft and munitions factories, "Rosie the Riveter" and her fellow war-plant veterans learned manual skills and technical expertise. The military programs recruited thousands of men into the U.S. Navy Seabees and the Army Corps of Engineers, and trained them in large-scale construction using cheap and quick prefabrication techniques.[3]

ON THE BATTLEFRONT AND FAR FROM HOME, American soldiers learned to be resourceful and inventive when confronted with Spartan living conditions. The experience of "making do" at military camps in Europe, North Africa, and the South Pacific accustomed GIs to "scrounging" and "cooking up" temporary residences with whatever they could find. They endured the war by converting packing crates

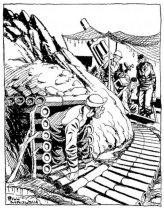

"Fire two more fer effect, Joe. I'm makin' a stovepipe."

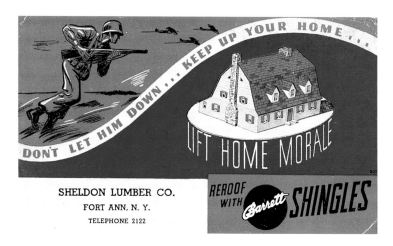

SHELDON LUMBER CO.
FORT ANN, N. Y.
TELEPHONE 2122

The Age of Do-It-Yourself

In any suburb any weekend, the master of the house is apt to turn into his own handyman. He's painting the porch, patching a pipe, or building an open-air fireplace so he can roast weenies in the garden.
"THE NEW DO-IT-YOURSELF MARKET," *BUSINESS WEEK*, JUNE 14, 1952[1]

World War II and its social and economic legacy accelerated the growth of the emerging home-improvement infrastructure and launched a widespread do-it-yourself craze in the United States. The war provided men and women with technical skills, confidence, and a predisposition toward using their resourcefulness to realize their dreams of domestic living. It exposed Americans at home and abroad to new materials and construction techniques. When the postwar economic boom placed homeownership within the reach of most middle-class families, conditions were ripe for do-it-yourself home improvement to come of age and become integrated into daily domestic life across a wide social spectrum.

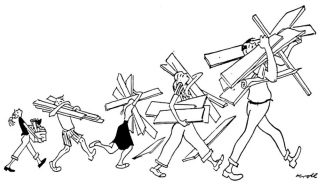

Cartoon by Julius Kroll, 1953

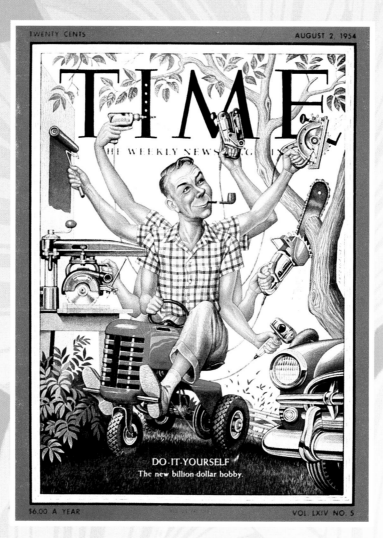

TOP Cover of *Time*, August 2,
1954

PREVIOUS PAGE Neighbors helping
to paint the Newtown, Connecticut
home of Mr. and Mrs. Harold
Steck, 1943

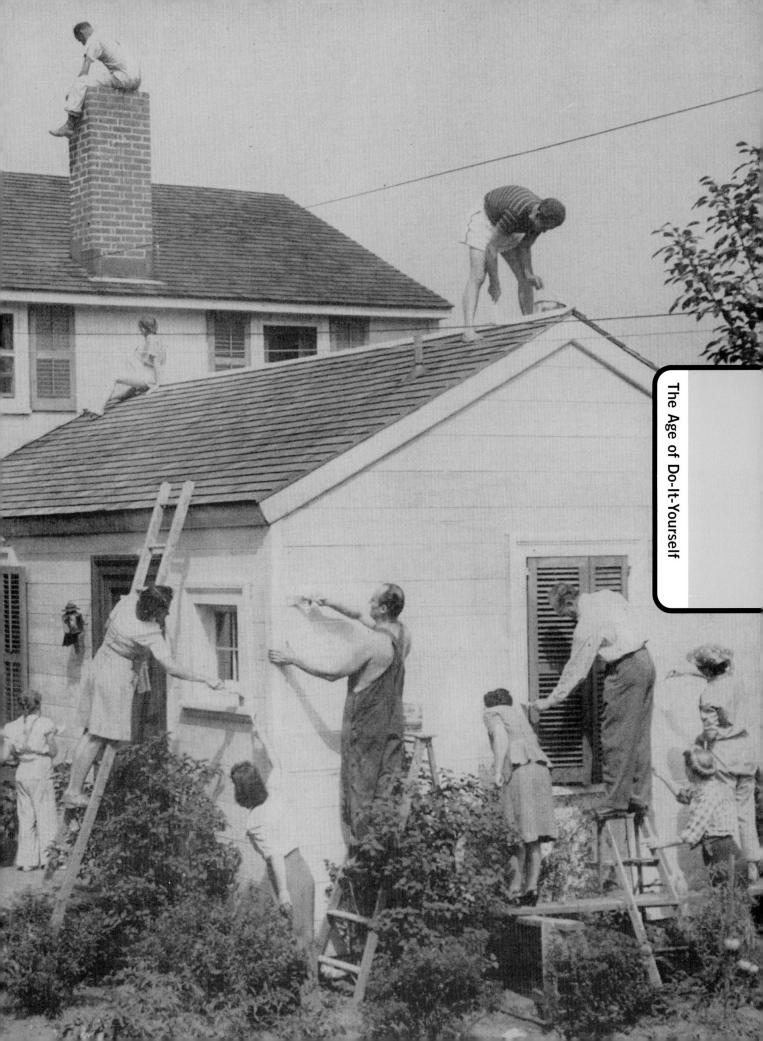

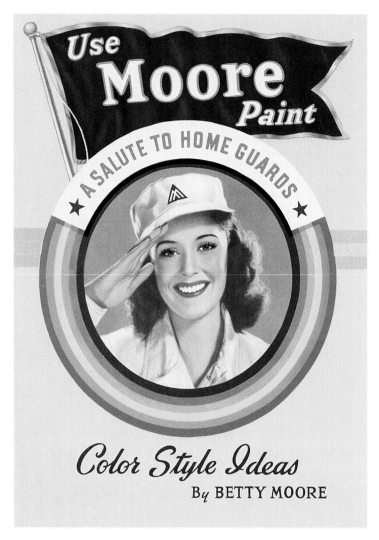

CLOCKWISE FROM LEFT

Benjamin Moore's decorating advisor Betty Moore called homeowners to action in protecting the home front, appearing on the front cover of *Color Style Ideas*, 1942.

Manufacturers promised that with the help of such products as Royledge paper shelving, any homemaker could apply wartime standards of efficiency and thrift to upgrading her home, 1943.

U.S. Employment Service recruitment poster aimed at women, ca. 1942

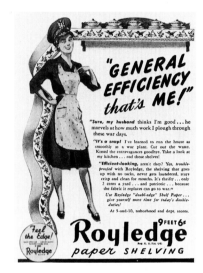

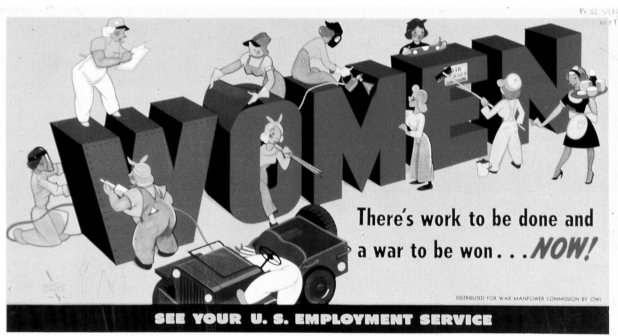

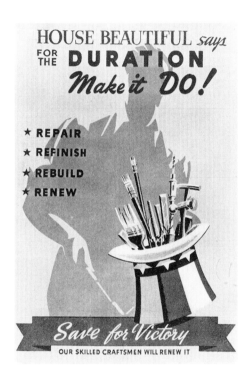

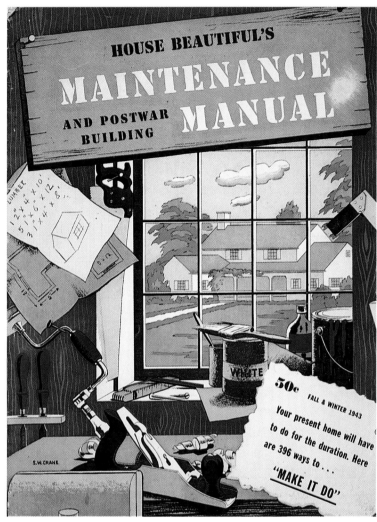

into floors and roofs, tin cans into smokestacks, and bomb cases into furniture. Because of these experiences, *House Beautiful* predicted that servicemen would come home from the war with not only the ability but also the desire to improve their surroundings.[4]

AT HOME, PATRIOTIC CAMPAIGNS urged American homemakers to conserve scarce resources and maintain their homes in the name of victory. *American Home* sounded a call to its readers to "repair for defense." Rather than encouraging consumers to spend, manufacturers and home-magazine editors taught them to "make it do" while the war was on and used advertisements to whet their appetites for peacetime when the "products of our future greatness" would benefit civilians. Publications such as *House Beautiful's Maintenance and Postwar Building Manual* gave tips on basic repairs while professionals were away on duty. Its concluding section offered "study courses" in home planning which encouraged readers to think about the possibilities of postwar living.[5]

Suburbanization

AFTER WORLD WAR II, economic prosperity made the dream of suburban living possible for unprecedented numbers of Americans. New house construction increased dramatically, and federal housing policy channeled this boom toward creating suburban developments. More than five million houses were built between 1946 and 1949. Residents owned an increasing proportion of these houses, with fifty-one percent of all dwelling units occupied by owners in 1950, as compared to forty-four percent in 1940. By 1959, thirty-one million of a total of forty-four million American families owned their own homes.[7] The growth in homeownership was due in large part to the GI Bill of Rights, passed by Congress toward the end of the war to ease soldiers' return to civilian life. This legislation enhanced the Federal Housing Administration loan system and made homeownership and suburban living accessible to a broader class spectrum than ever before. GIs could obtain home mortgages with little or no down payment. In 1947 the GI Bill granted more than 800,000 housing loans to veterans. Two years later, veterans constituted nearly half of the nation's total number of new home buyers. By 1961, 5.6 million housing loans were recorded for World War II and Korean War veterans, and sixty percent of American families owned their own homes.[8]

GOVERNMENT LOANS SUBSIDIZED the construction of cheap, affordable homes in suburban settings. With the help of the FHA, real-estate developers who had pioneered the speculative building of small homes in the 1920s and 1930s applied quantity-production techniques to build large numbers of "starter homes" after the war. Many of the new suburban homes were simple in design and construction, leaving lots of room for home improvement. For example, the early low-cost homes in William and Alfred Levitt's famous Levittown developments in Pennsylvania and New York, built in 1947 and 1948, featured staircases leading up to unfinished attics.[9]

THE RANCH-STYLE HOUSES built in Levittown's second phase of development (1949–1951) contained even more possibilities for home improvement, including a rear window in the living room that could be removed to make way for a door to an additional room. Carports could be enclosed as garages or converted into living space. Levitt's promotional materials encouraged remodeling and, indeed, Levittown residents altered their dwellings to suit their stylistic preferences and their expanding families.[10]

WITH MARRIAGE AND BIRTH RATES ON THE RISE, the new homeowners of the postwar era were primarily young families. Two surveys revealed that the median age of new home buyers in 1950 was 35,

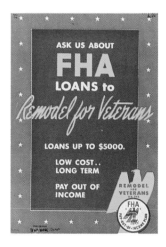

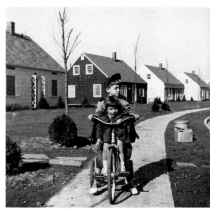

FAR TOP **FHA** poster announcing the availability of home-remodeling loans for veterans, 1945–46

TOP Jefferson and Suellen Smith on Stone Lane, Levittown, New York, in the late 1940s

and that they tended to be married with children. Having previously settled for rental apartments in the cities, these families were eager to own their first homes. They also wanted more living space, both indoors and out. Four out of ten buyers interviewed expressed dissatisfaction with the number of rooms in their new home. The surveys also revealed that seventy percent of the new home buyers had saved money to make improvements immediately after they moved in. Sixty-two percent of all home buyers reported having done some of the work themselves, while twenty-three percent claimed to have done all or most of it on their own.[11] Do-it-yourself home improvement held the promise of realizing dreams of middle-class identity for these first-time homeowners, many of whom had been raised in working-class families and exposed to manual skills during the war.

Do It Yourself

THE SUBURBAN IDEAL, and the postwar building boom that made it accessible to growing numbers of Americans, provided a context for do-it-yourself to become a mass cultural phenomenon in the early 1950s. Popular magazines proclaimed the trend's arrival. "This is the age of do-it-yourself," *Business Week* announced.[13] While the possibilities for do-it-yourself home improvement had been emerging for several decades, it now

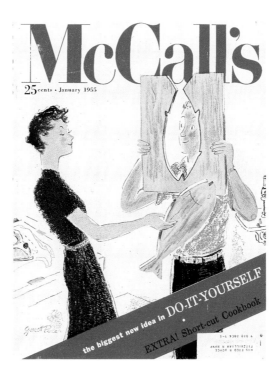

Cover of *McCall's*,
January 1955

became an acceptable, desirable, and even expected activity for large numbers of American families.

ON THE MOST BASIC LEVEL, do-it-yourself was a response to economic and labor-market conditions of the immediate postwar era. A shortage of skilled labor encouraged homeowners — especially veterans and industrial workers who had acquired technical skills during the war — to improve their homes with their own two hands. Doing their own repairs also saved homeowners the cost of hiring professionals, and regular maintenance eliminated the need to pay for large jobs later on. *Business Week* identified the high cost of labor as the "overwhelming, immediate reason" that homeowners took on remodeling projects in their spare time.[14]

BUT THE APPEAL OF DO-IT-YOURSELF TRANSCENDED cost-benefit analysis. For many American families, home-improvement activities provided a way of obtaining the house and lifestyle to which they aspired—a way of participating in the American dream. Do-it-yourself resonated as a quintessential expression of that dream, especially as it was defined by the dominant values of the 1950s: domesticity, leisure, and independence.

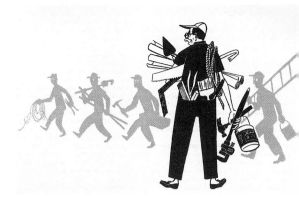

TOP Cartoon from *Changing Times, the Kiplinger Magazine*, 1953

BOTTOM A typical knotty-pine-paneled 1950s basement recreation room and home workshop, as conceived by Armstrong, manufacturers of asphalt floor tile, 1952. A Shopsmith five-in-one combination woodworking tool sits in the middle background.

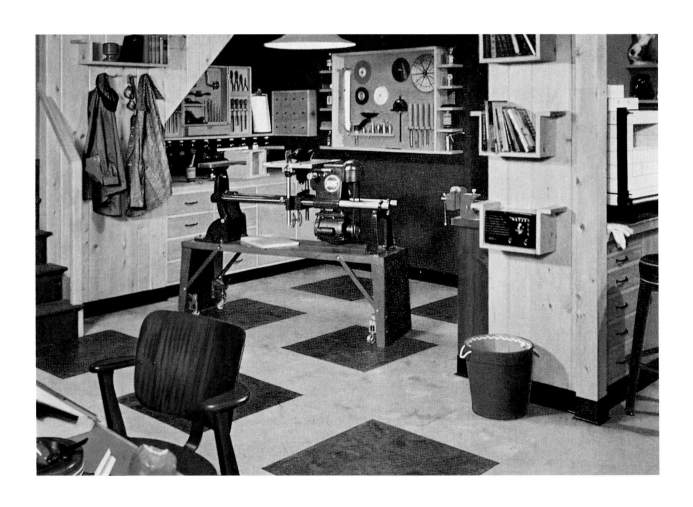

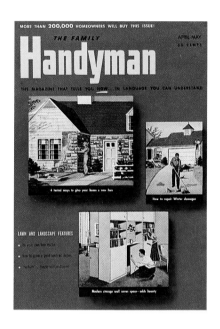

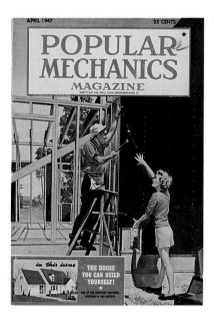

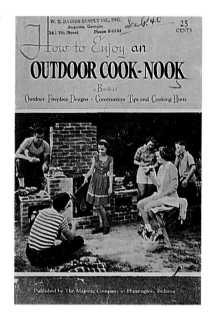

Cover of *The Family Handyman*, April/May 1952

Responding to the postwar interest in amateur construction and renovation, *Popular Mechanics* commissioned plans for a "Build-It-Yourself House," then followed the efforts of twenty-three-year-old veteran Jacques Brownson to build it, 1947.

Cover of *How to Enjoy an Outdoor Cook-Nook*, 1949

THE DO-IT-YOURSELF ETHOS was well-suited to the era's emphasis on domesticity. Contemporary surveys showed a dramatic rise in the proportion of the nation's wealth being spent on home pursuits in the Cold War period. Historian Elaine Tyler May has characterized this era as one of "virtuous consumerism," in which spending reinforced a family-centered way of life. She writes, "Americans responded [to the Cold War] with guarded optimism by making purchases that would strengthen their sense of security. In the postwar years, investing in one's own home, along with the trappings that would presumably enhance family life, was seen as the best way to plan for the future."[15] For many families, do-it-yourself home improvement was an economical way to upgrade their dwellings according to the middle-class standards of the day.

AN EMERGING CULTURE OF LEISURE DEFINED the home as a place of relaxation. After the war, the forty-hour work week became the norm, leaving time for two-day weekends. Union contracts included paid vacations and set a standard in the workplace for others to follow. Middle-class Americans expected to spend free time at home doing things that were pleasurable and relaxing. The quest for fun led many American families to embrace outdoor living and to pursue projects, such as building outdoor barbecues, that contributed to a culture of backyard togetherness and entertaining.[16]

DO-IT-YOURSELF ALSO SEEMED TO REPRESENT independence from the corporate world. Popular writers grounded the do-it-yourself idea in the American past by linking it to Yankee ingenuity and an imagined agrarian, democratic past. They invoked Henry David Thoreau as the "patron saint of the theoretical do-it-yourself-man."[17]

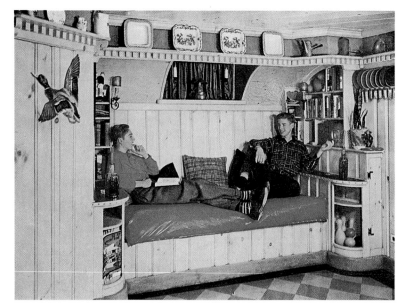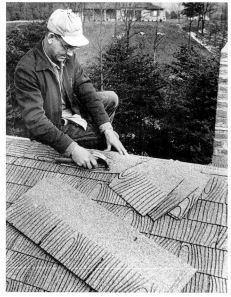

The association with the values of liberty and freedom reinforced Cold War anti-Communist rhetoric. And a focus on individualism seemed, in the eyes of social critics, to function as an antidote to the monotony of corporate office work and to the conformity imposed by mass culture.[18] As artist Lucille Corcos wrote in a 1955 *McCall's* article accompanying her lively illustration of do-it-yourselfers enthusiastically transforming the suburban landscape, "Maybe it's creative therapy for the world we live in—getting down to basic problems you and your family can solve together with your hands."[19]

THE VALUES OF DOMESTICITY, leisure, and independence permeated the era's burgeoning array of how-to literature. Already in the business of telling people how to do things around the house, home-magazine editors encouraged remodeling projects with new zeal. *Popular Mechanics* shifted its focus to include more home-improvement articles as well as additional illustrated "step-by-step" building projects for amateurs. This shift corresponded to a dramatic increase in circulation between 1945 and 1946 from 750,000 to 1,000,000 readers.[20] A new magazine, *Family Handyman*, was launched in 1951 to respond to the public's growing desire to be "handy." By showing readers how to perform various tasks and helping them navigate the expanding marketplace, these publications reinforced the do-it-yourself trend.

THE POPULARITY OF MAGAZINE ARTICLES promoting do-it-yourself provided an incentive for the publication of a new wave of books and instruction manuals aimed at the absolute novice. Through easy-to-use formats and extensive photographic illustrations, these how-to publications addressed nonspecialists more deliberately than

TOP **A man in the suburbs of Charleston, South Carolina installing asphalt shingles on his roof, 1954**

TOP LEFT **A corner of the recreation room created by G. V. Fuller for his family's home in Englewood, New Jersey, 1942**

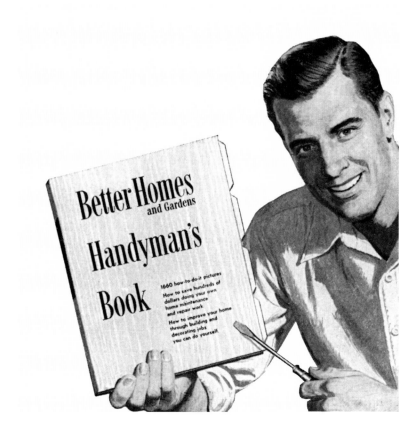

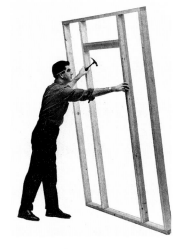

their early-20th-century predecessors had. The *Better Homes and Gardens Handyman's Book*, first published in 1951, aimed "to provide basic know-how, as clearly and simply as possible, for the average man who putters around, just keeping his house in comfortable working order."[21] An introductory section listed basic hand tools all homeowners should own and gave instruction on how to use them. More than 1,500 step-by-step pictures showed such tasks as "how to use a hammer" and "how to build a workbench." The book emphasized home repairs and improvements that required little or no skill. It told how to make minor plumbing and electrical repairs, but stopped short of providing instructions on how to install such systems in their entirety. Paneling with plywood, building storage units, and laying flooring were among the most complicated projects included.

THE BOOK'S LOOSE-LEAF BINDER FORMAT REFLECTED and reinforced the notions of individuality and self-sufficiency behind do-it-yourself. Readers could update the book's contents with their own notes or additional pages from the monthly *Better Homes and Gardens* magazine. A tab system separating each chapter made the book practical and easy to consult "with a flick of your finger." *Better Homes and Gardens*'s editors promised the users of this manual not only

savings on repair bills but also respite from "a troubled world." Whether they found relief, satisfaction, or frustration, readers bought the manual in large quantities, propelling the book to number five on the nonfiction bestseller list in its first year.[22] The sales of books like this one took off in the 1950s and 1960s, a success that indicated the great degree to which Americans embraced do-it-yourself home improvement.

Spoofing the Amateur

DO-IT-YOURSELF SOON BECAME the subject of jokes and popular humor; to cartoonists in particular, it seemed a ripe topic for ridicule and commentary. Morris Brickman even named his syndicated comic panel *Do It Yourself*. In their explorations of domestic life in postwar America, Brickman and his fellow humorists seized on the home-improvement trend as an expression of suburban dreams and realities, and the values of postwar culture. Not knowing quite what to make of do-it-yourself, they tackled the question of why it had captivated so many people seemingly overnight. These cartoons celebrated the enthusiasm with which Americans engaged in home improvement and repairs, but also highlighted the naiveté with which much of this activity was undertaken. MANY CARTOONS SITUATED DO-IT-YOURSELF in a confusing netherworld between work and play. On the one hand, home-improvement projects held promises of respite and escape from office routines. On the other hand, the pressure and drive to successfully complete tasks could quickly transform what was "only a hobby" into a serious job. Brickman's homeowners spent their "free" time hard at work. THE INCOMPETENCE OF THE AMATEUR HANDYMAN was another predominant theme in these cartoons. Homeowners used the wrong tools, chose inappropriate materials, and became easily overwhelmed by projects that were too ambitious — sometimes literally painting themselves into corners. One of the era's most pointed satires came from Bill Mauldin, a cartoonist who had developed a popular following during World War II through his coverage of soldiers on the battlefront. Turning his attention to civilian life after 1945, Mauldin published an illustrated article in *Life* magazine entitled "How Do-It-Yourself Amateurs Are Clobbering Themselves." Characterizing do-it-yourself as an out-of-control fad that trapped homeowners in a web of unsafe, futile practices, Mauldin portrayed a handyman husband "polishing his own gutters" while a runaway lawn mower plowed into his supporting ladder and strangled him with the cord of his electric drill.[24] Not surprisingly, the piece sparked the ire of *Family*

It probably took no more than four years off John Drone's normal life expectancy to build that outdoor fireplace, but such are the occupational hazards of do-it-yourself.
JOHN KEATS, *THE CRACK IN THE PICTURE WINDOW*, 1956[23]

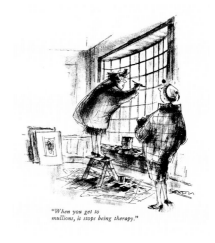

"When you get to mullions, it stops being therapy."

Cartoon by Saxon from
***The New Yorker*, 1958**

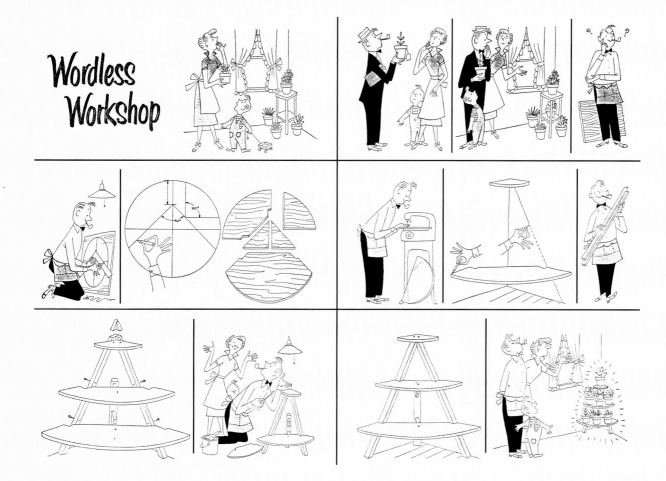

Cartoons

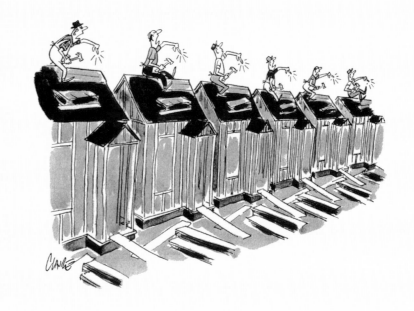

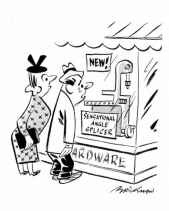

Every time I think my workshop is complete,
they throw something new at me!

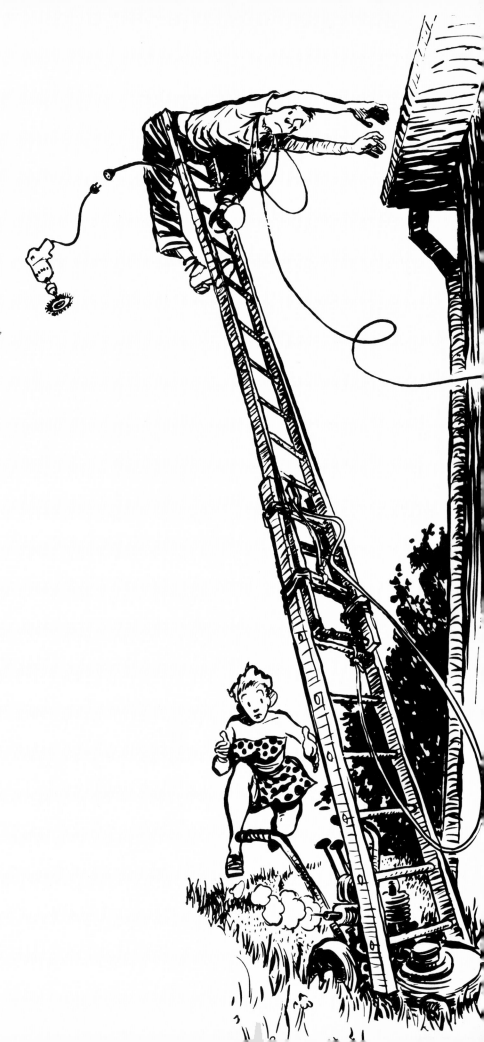

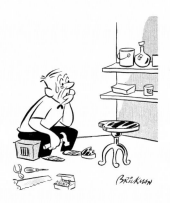

It's only a hobby...a hobby...
just a hobby...only a hobby...

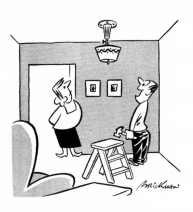

It's our old table lamp.

Handyman's editor, who came to the defense of do-it-yourself later that year in his own magazine.[25]

OTHER CARTOONS CALLED ATTENTION to the silly or spurious ingenuity that often lay behind the decade's home-improvement activity. Instructional books and magazines suggested projects that ranged from the practical to the ridiculous, and humorists helped do-it-yourselfers laugh at the degree to which they were at the mercy of expert advisers. "Wordless Workshop," a regular feature of *Popular Science* magazines, incorporated how-to literature's visual techniques in a narrative spoof of its overly clever ideas. In one Brickman cartoon, a couple installed a table lamp on a ceiling.

AS A SEEMINGLY ENDLESS ARRAY of home-improvement tools and supplies was introduced, many cartoons portrayed amateur builders as adrift in the expanding marketplace. Eager hardware-store salesmen were depicted as the source of enthusiasm for do-it-yourself. Other cartoons mocked the notion that do-it-yourself was simply a matter of buying the right product, and that the correct tools could make anyone "handy." And they made fun of the idea that the mere purchase of tool kits and building supplies would generate the "joy of creating."

IN SPOOFING THE MARKETPLACE, cartoons drove home the point that do-it-yourselfers were not independent homesteaders but members of modern industrial society. Do-it-yourself was part of the consumer culture in which homeowners were enmeshed, and amateur remodelers relied on the offerings of the marketplace when they undertook any kind of repair or remodeling project. Their drive to rebuild, adjust, and tinker with their dwellings presented vast marketing opportunities for manufacturers and retailers.

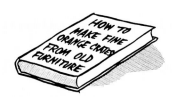

From Morris Brickman,
Do It Yourself, 1955

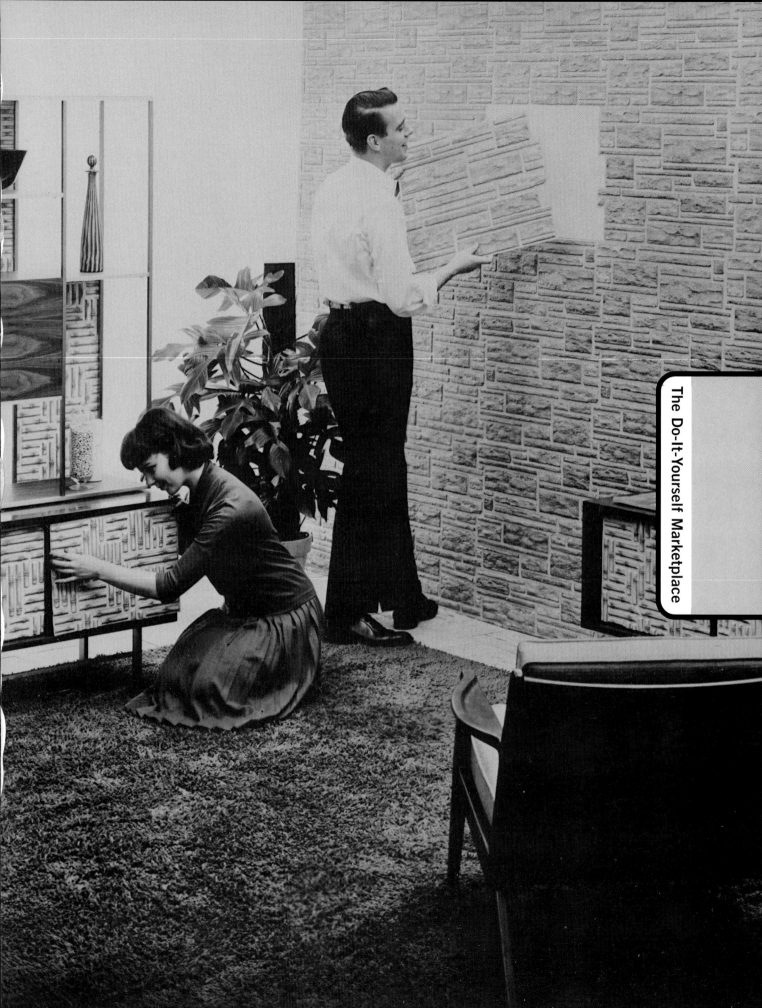

This Christmas suggest

$169⁵⁰ complete
except for motor.
With special, ½-hp., ball-
bearing, heavy-duty motor
(shown) ... $199⁵⁰

TOP The Shopsmith combi-
nation tool, 1950

PREVIOUS PAGE Do-it-yourself
installation of faux-stone wall
covering and coordinating tile,
ca. 1960

The Do-It-Yourself Marketplace

The popular interest in do-it-yourself—and the enthusiasm for home remodeling it generated—revolutionized the design and retailing of building materials, tools, and other supplies. Although many manufacturers and dealers had begun to develop and market tools and materials for do-it-yourselfers in the early decades of the century, they responded most seriously to these potential customers only after 1945. During the postwar period, as part of an overall effort to convert wartime manufacturing facilities to peacetime uses, many industrial leaders redesigned and repackaged their products to meet the needs of amateur builders interested in changing or upgrading their homes. The transformed marketplace expanded the possibilities for do-it-yourself amateurs and raised expectations for the types of projects homeowners could take on. Many new products had professional skills designed and built into them. Widely available in self-service hardware stores and home centers, these products placed large and small repair and remodeling tasks within the grasp of nonspecialists. As products such as power tools, paint rollers, and drywall became everyday household supplies, do-it-yourselfers began to master increasingly ambitious and sophisticated home-improvement projects.

Paneling a room with plywood is one of the most exciting jobs you can do in your home. It is exciting because so much can be done to make a room handsome with little skill and time.
BETTER HOMES AND GARDENS
HANDYMAN'S BOOK, 1951[1]

TO RIDE THE WAVE OF POSTWAR PROSPERITY and attract the business of American homeowners, manufacturers began redesigning building tools and supplies soon after 1945. Traditionally, the hardware industry had addressed the needs of professionals and specialists in the building trades. In seeking a mass market for their goods, producers of repair and construction supplies marketed directly to the do-it-yourselfer by providing products and kits that greatly simplified projects and repairs. Amateur-friendly tools, often packaged with accessories and manuals offering detailed instructions and project suggestions, substituted for the hired specialist and made it possible for amateurs to tackle tasks that had once been out of reach. To make these products more accessible and inviting to novices, manufacturers packaged them in bright colors and gave them special names to associate them with domesticity and infuse them with the do-it-yourself spirit.

THE DEMANDS OF WAR had led many manufacturing firms to develop new tools, techniques, and synthetic materials. Now they applied this knowledge to adapting industrial-purpose tools and machinery for home use. At trade shows and in industry publications, producers conferred about how to redirect the hardware industry to attract the attention of the nation's growing number of homeowners. The National Hardware Show, established in 1946, provided a forum for manufacturers and retailers to work together to develop new ways of designing for and marketing to amateur builders. Within a few short years, the hardware industry's new orientation had caught the attention of the business and popular press, which heralded the arrival of a do-it-yourself market. The dramatic rise in sales of a variety of hand-held electric tools for amateurs was an early indicator. Before the war, the power-tool industry had total sales of $25 million; by 1954 sales

RIGHT "Koiled Kords" product demonstration using irons and telephones at the 1946 National Hardware Show

FAR RIGHT Retailers and trade representatives register at the National Hardware Show, 1954.

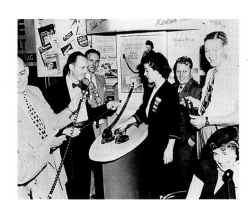

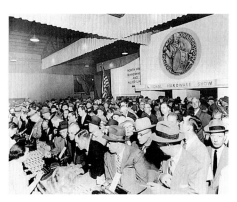

climbed to $200 million. Whereas less than two dozen different types of power tools were available for home use in 1940, *Business Week* counted about a hundred in 1952.[2]

THE ELECTRIC DRILL was one of the first industrial-purpose tools to become a staple of home workshops. Several companies had attempted to sell power drills to farmers and amateurs before the war, but only after 1945 did they find a sizable market for this product. Black & Decker's quarter-inch power drill was one of the earliest successes. According to company lore, Black & Decker managers discovered the potential market when they noticed that many of their employees took industrial-purpose drills home with them to make repairs and alterations to their houses. To reach the consumer market, Black & Decker packaged these tools in brightly colored boxes, advertised in national magazines, and began distribution through department stores, appliance dealers, and hardware stores. In 1949, the company launched a new series of drills and other power tools under the name "Home-Utility Electric Tools."[3] Other manufacturers soon introduced similar products and marketing strategies. Within a few years, Skil introduced a "Skil Home Shop Tool" line of hand-held power drills and saws, and Porter-Cable launched a campaign for its competing products under the brand name "Homemaster."[4]

TO PROMOTE THE ELECTRIC DRILL'S USEFULNESS for a variety of tasks, manufacturers packaged it in special boxes or kits with accessories. Attachments could turn a drill into a sander, a grinder, or a polishing wheel for buffing wood or metal surfaces. According to advertisements, the drill could be put to use in almost any home project. Electric drill kits were explicitly designed for the generalist

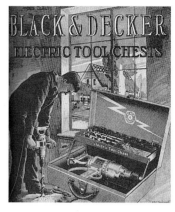

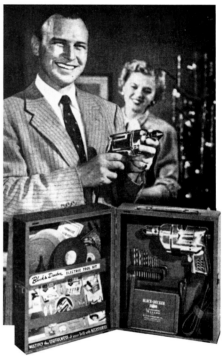

FAR TOP The manufacturers of early electric tools aimed their advertising primarily at professional contractors, 1928.

TOP An electric drill and its accessories, packaged together in an "all-in-one" kit, 1953

LEFT A Dremel electric sander and its suggested uses, 1949

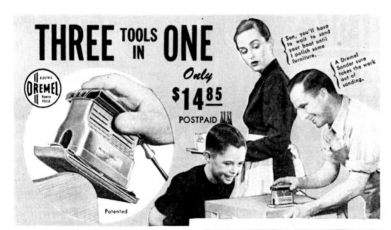

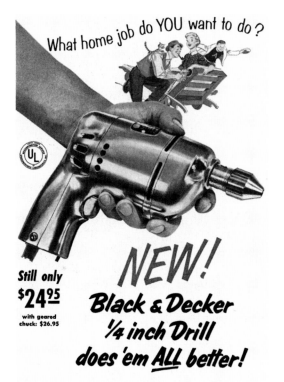

What home job do YOU want to do?

Still only $24⁹⁵
with geared chuck: $26.95

NEW!
Black & Decker
¼ inch Drill
does 'em ALL better!

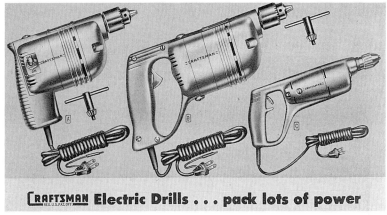

CRAFTSMAN Electric Drills . . . pack lots of power

Just squeeze the trigger for any speed from 0 to 2000 rpm.

PICK OF THE PROS

SKIL
POWER TOOLS

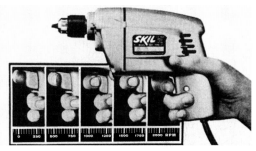

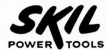

CLOCKWISE FROM TOP LEFT

An advertising image of a
Black & Decker quarter-inch
electric drill, 1955

Three Craftsman quarter-inch drill
models, 1949

A Skil electric drill with trigger
speed control, 1965

who used each attachment on an occasional basis only. The potential versatility of the electric hand drill led one commentator to characterize it as "a motorized shop you can hold in your hand."[5]

GENERAL-PURPOSE COMBINATION TOOLS capable of performing multiple tasks took the idea of the portable workshop a step further. The Shopsmith, introduced in 1947, was a five-in-one tool marketed to homeowners who may not have already owned any power woodworking equipment. Its features included a circular saw, a drill press, a wood lathe, a disc sander, and a horizontal drill. Although it was less expensive than buying each tool separately, the Shopsmith required readjustment for each operation. Initially available only through Montgomery Ward stores, Shopsmith sold over 50,000 units in two years.[6] Other multipurpose tools on the market included the Deltashop, intended for "the ten-thumbed men who don't know a kerf from a miter."[7]

THEIR INITIAL SUCCESS in marketing these tools led manufacturers to offer new products with an even greater array of features. To make electric hand tools appear sleek and modern like other household appliances, manufacturers designed many of them in the same streamlined style used in refrigerators and toasters. The Shopsmith's 1954 Mark V model had a shiny, painted metal surface with smooth, rounded edges. Its moving parts were covered to make them safer.[8] The designs of many other power tools were also adapted to make

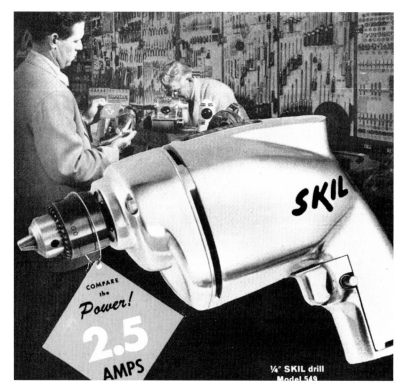

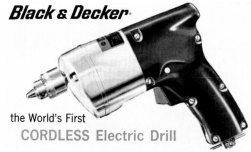

the World's First
CORDLESS Electric Drill

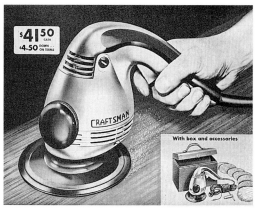

them lighter, more attractive, and easier to handle. Cordless drills, although expensive and underpowered at first, were introduced in the early 1960s. Later drills featured a reversing switch that eased the difficulty of removing the bit from the wood. Together these types of features made the electric drill an everyday household object by the 1970s.

NEW MATERIALS ALSO WIDENED the possibilities for do-it-yourselfers in the immediate postwar years. The building boom and materials shortage during and after World War II had led builders to adopt plywood as a standard construction material.[9] Made of layers of wood laminated tightly together, plywood was cheap, workable, and versatile. Usually sold in standardized four-by-eight-foot panels, the material was suitable for house construction but was difficult to cut with a handsaw for smaller projects. By the early 1950s, the Douglas Fir Plywood Association began marketing smaller pieces of plywood for the home carpenter under the brand name "Handy Panels," as well as prefinished panels for a variety of decorative effects.[10] With these innovations, plywood became a mainstay of do-it-yourself home improvement.

MANUFACTURERS REPACKAGED and marketed other industrial building materials to the amateur builder. In 1953, the Reynolds Metals Company introduced "Do-It-Yourself Aluminum," which could be cut with a woodsaw and assembled into stair railings, fences, and

CLOCKWISE FROM TOP LEFT

Skil Corporation's version of the quarter-inch drill, 1957

A Black & Decker cordless electric drill, 1961

A Craftsman disc sander, 1949

awnings.[11] Homeowners could also buy insulation in square blocks
for easy installation. Alterations to gypsum wallboard made it lighter
and cheaper and useful in a wide range of home-improvement
projects. Precut materials packaged in kits with necessary tools and
accessories made it possible for novices to familiarize themselves
with an expanding array of construction materials.

BY THE 1970S, manufacturers combined innovations in materials with
the practice of marketing kits for amateurs to bring plumbing and
electrical work into the domain of homeowners. Manufacturers of
plumbing and electrical supplies turned to the do-it-yourself market
after 1960 with the introduction of plastic piping and plastic-coated
electrical cable, which made technically demanding tasks more
accessible to amateurs. Electricians had traditionally installed or
repaired electrical systems using heavy metal-sheathed wire cable that
required a hacksaw to cut. The introduction of nonmetallic sheathed
cable in the early 1960s—commonly known by the brand name
Romex—made it possible for the do-it-yourselfer to accomplish small
wiring projects. This plastic-coated wire bent easily and could be cut
with a wire cutter. Where local building codes allowed it, homeowners
could now add an extra outlet with some wiring know-how gleaned
from do-it-yourself manuals. By the mid-1970s, amateur handypeople
regularly used nonmetallic sheathed cable to make their own
repairs.[12] Manufacturers developed other electrical products and kits
aimed at the amateur market, such as the prewired "Uinstal" outdoor
electrical outlet.[13]

BEFORE 1970, only minor plumbing repairs, such as fixing a leaky
faucet, were considered to be within the amateur's grasp. Although
home-improvement articles in the early 1950s showcased plumbing
repair and addition projects using copper tubing, home plumbing
did not truly enter the realm of do-it-yourself until the introduction
of plastic polyvinyl chloride (PVC) piping in the late 1960s. PVC pipe
made plumbing additions and repairs possible with just a small
saw, or, in the case of flexible piping, with a kitchen knife. If a
homeowner made a mistake, however, the irreversible glue used to
fasten the plastic piping required readhering those pipe sections
all over again.

BY THE 1970S, undertaking repair and remodeling work on one's
own had become so commonplace that even some of the most
technically challenging home-improvement projects could be accom-
plished by amateurs.

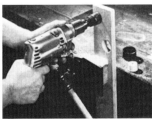

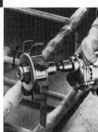

Portable electric
drill *continued*

Sawing. Hole-saw attachments like this will
cut holes up to two inches in diameter neatly
and quickly. A small guide drill in the center
helps you locate holes accurately. You can also
get a small circular saw attachment for your
drill. Still another attachment converts rotary
action to back-and-forth action. It holds stiff
saw blades that will make straight or pattern
cuts in wood, metal, linoleum, wallboard.

Sanding. A sanding attachment for your elec- ➤
tric drill will save you many hours of hand-
work. The merry-go-round gadget on the drill
at right is one of the more unusual of the attachments you can buy for sanding. Bristles
project from the rim to support strips of abrasive cloth, which may be turned out and
clipped off as they become worn. Because of
its flexible brushes, it sands irregular surfaces.

➤ **Sanding drums.** The kit pictured will ease
small jobs of grinding and smoothing. It contains abrasive-paper sleeves with various grit
sizes to suit the job at hand, plus a series of
small sanding drums you can clamp in the
drill's chuck. In the background is a rotary-
action converter with a flexible rubber backing, to which you can cement sandpaper.

Flat sander. This flat-sanding attachment ➤
converts the natural rotary action of the drill
to an oscillating motion for sanding. It does
an extremely smooth finishing job, polishes
wax, too. It has quickly detachable pads
sized to hold sections cut from regular sheets
of abrasive paper or cloth, depending on job.

454

CLOCKWISE FROM TOP

Given the right attachments,
homeowners could use the
portable electric drill for multiple
jobs, including sawing holes,
sanding, polishing, scraping, and
hedge-trimming, 1951.

Preformed plywood wall panels
such as Weldwood's Plankweld
were a staple of do-it-yourself
home improvement, 1951.

Family members installing their
own insulation, from a Gold Bond
Twinsulation advertisement, 1956

Do-it-yourself aluminum advertisement, from the Reynolds Metals
Company, 1953

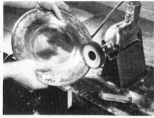

Cleaning. Removing tarnish from silverware, jewelry, or brass is an easy job for the drill. Use a rag buffing wheel plus a polishing compound for a bright finish without scratches. The inexpensive horizontal stand shown holds the drill firmly and frees both hands for guiding the work. Peg in the handle of the drill locks trigger so motor runs until the trigger is released.

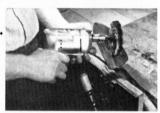

Scraping. To whisk away rust, scale, oil paint, or even to clean up that fire-blackened coffeepot, check upon the numerous brush accessories available for your hand drill. Here, a coarse wire brush cleans a rusted garden trowel. Finer wire brushes can be used to put a satin finish on metals or to clean stubborn spill-overs from the kitchen range.

Clipping. If you still are unconvinced that the drill is a versatile tool, this attachment should clinch the argument. It's a clipper that trims five feet of hedge per minute, and all you have to do is guide it. Use guide strings on hedge to keep your clipping level. Use clipper only when the hedge is dry. Like any electric tool, drill does not take to water.

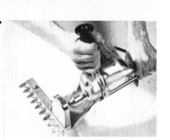

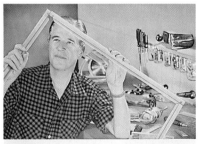

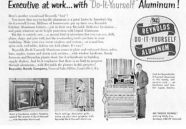

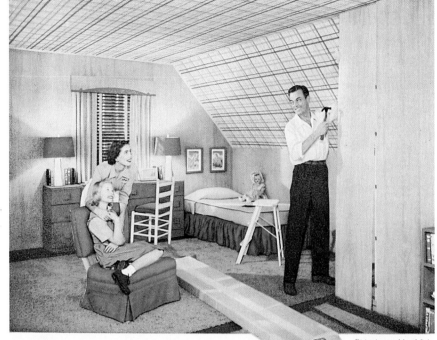

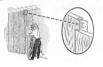

This ingenious, concealed metal clip is what holds Plankweld firmly to the wall and makes it so easy to put up. You can even nail right into plaster, without worrying over stud locations and without fussing.

Build this wood-paneled room

in your expansion attic

for as little as $249.50†

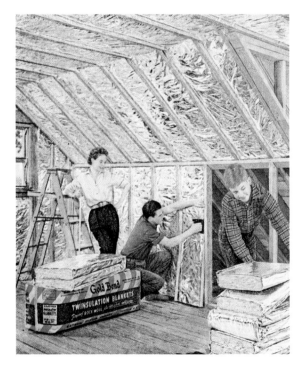

Painting and Decorating

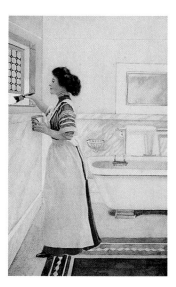

A homemaker or maid painting window trim, probably using a quick-drying enamel paint, from the *Acme Quality Painting Guide Book*, ca. 1910

THE MANUFACTURING AND MARKETING OF PAINT, wallpaper, and floor coverings similarly transformed painting and interior decorating from professional remodeling tasks into projects suitable for the amateur. New types of equipment aimed at nonspecialists moved the jobs of refinishing walls, floors, and ceilings from the exclusive province of contractors to the domain of homeowners in the decade between 1945 and 1955.

DO-IT-YOURSELF PAINTING had been an option for many homeowners from the last half of the 19th century onward, but it was relatively uncommon for families outside rural areas to mix their own paint, or even to use the increasingly available ready-mixed paints to cover anything bigger than a chair, a window frame, or a porch. Early-20th-century paint manufacturers marketed many enamels, varnishes, and water-thinned calcimines to amateurs for such small projects, but they assumed that homeowners would hire professional painters for the complicated process of mixing and applying oil-and-lead house paints.

SHORTAGES OF LEAD AND OIL during World War II, coupled with a desire to circumvent the influence of professional painters and create new markets, led manufacturers in the 1940s to focus development and marketing energies on water-based resin emulsion paints that could be easily used by homeowners. The National Chemical and Manufacturing Company's Ultra Luminall and Sherwin-Williams's Kem-Tone were among the first such brands on the market.[15] Emulsion paints—which after 1949 used latex as their main binder—covered plaster, old paint, and wallpaper in one coat, without primers. They could be thinned and cleaned up with water, dried into washable yet colorfast films, and had little odor. Using them involved, as every Kem-Tone ad pointed out, "No muss, no fuss, no bother."[16]

MANUFACTURERS AGGRESSIVELY MARKETED these quintessentially do-it-yourself paints, making it easy for homeowners to know about them, buy them, and use them. For example, Sherwin-Williams assured that Kem-Tone could be bought virtually anywhere by abandoning the usual practice of distributing through exclusive dealers. It made Kem-Tone available to any retailer—gas station, drug store, grocery store—who wanted to enter the paint-selling business. So successful was Sherwin-Williams's marketing strategy that Kem-Tone sales doubled each year throughout the late 1940s.[17] As other manufacturers introduced similar paints and accessories, increasing numbers of homeowners did their own painting. By the early 1950s, surveys by home-improvement magazines

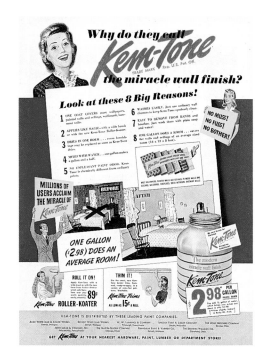

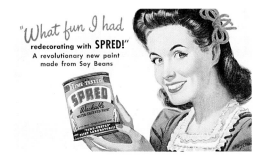

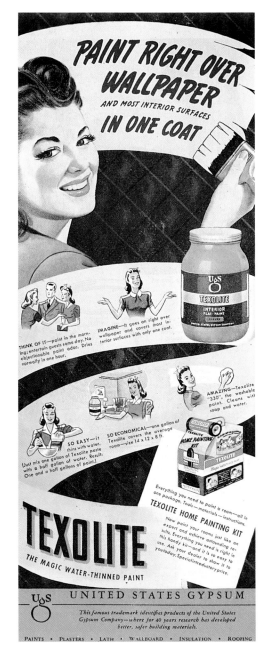

indicated that between seventy and ninety percent of readers did
their own painting.[18]

AN ADDITIONAL BOOST TO DO-IT-YOURSELF PAINTING came in the
form of the paint roller. Although first patented as early as 1869,
rollers only superseded brushes for wall painting after Sherwin-
Williams introduced its Kem-Decorator Roller-Koater as part of the
marketing campaign for its Kem-Tone resin-emulsion paint. The roller
was part of the company's integrated line of accessories and step-by-
step instructions designed and packaged in a coordinated yellow-
and-blue color scheme.[19]

THESE MERCHANDISING TECHNIQUES invited consumers to become
more involved not just in the act of painting, but also in the selection
of colors and decorating schemes—without the interference of professional painters. Before the war, companies had published paint and
color guides to show homeowners how to lend "color style" or "color
harmony" to their homes. After the war they went a step further and
marketed color through special in-store displays, where color guides
could be interpreted for the individual consumer by professional
decorators. To provide consumers with the widest range of colors while
at the same time keeping store stocks at manageable levels, numerous
companies developed automatic and manual colorant-dispensing
machines in the mid- to late-1950s. The Martin-Senour Company's
1957 Colorobot, for instance, held eight basic pigments that it mixed
using punch-card-encoded formulae to create any of 7,500 standard,
reproducible colors. With such devices, stores needed to stock

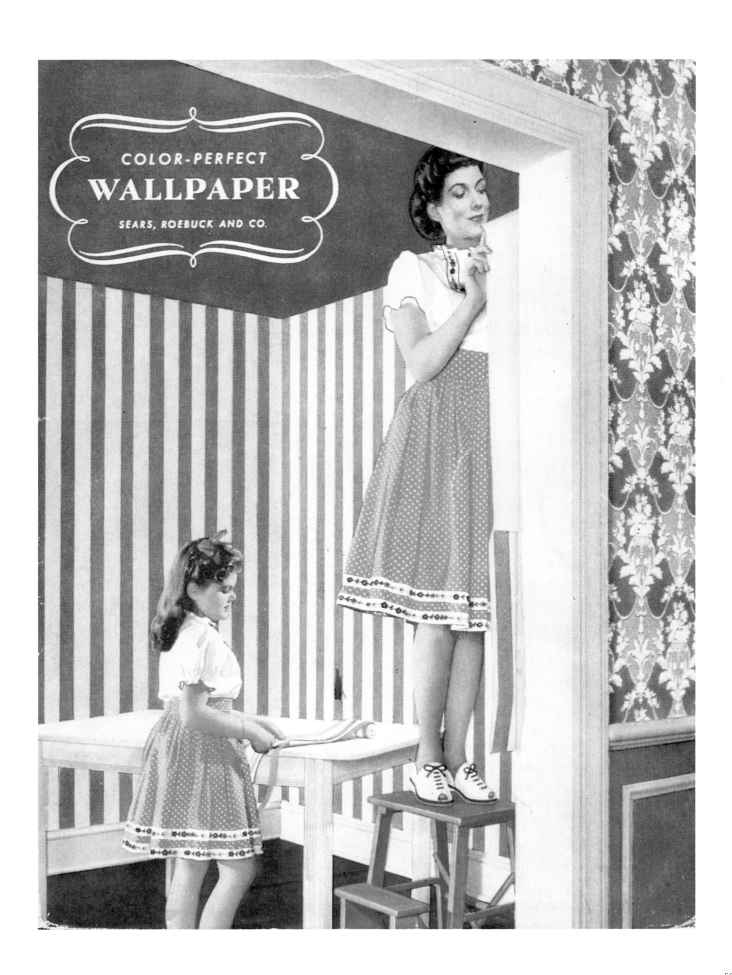

COLOR-PERFECT
WALLPAPER
SEARS, ROEBUCK AND CO.

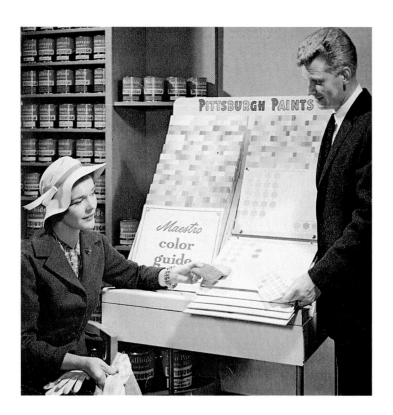

The Maestro Color Guide allowed prospective buyers of Pittsburgh Paints to explore decorative ideas about color, perhaps with the help of a knowledgeable salesperson, 1962.

only white bases and a few pigments to provide customers with any color they wanted, on demand.[20]

PAINT MANUFACTURERS BOASTED that their products could "paint right over wallpaper" easily and quickly. Indeed, the success of emulsion paints put pressure on wallpaper manufacturers to develop do-it-yourself equivalents of their products, as well as easy-to-use application systems. Hanging wallpaper was traditionally a skilled craft that required an array of specialized rulers, levels, knives, pastes, and brushes. During the war, United Wallpaper introduced TRIMZ, a prepasted, amateur-friendly wallcovering that eliminated the messy and difficult task of applying paste by hand. This more forgiving system featured slow-drying paste, which allowed amateurs to adjust or remove improperly positioned wallpaper. In the late 1940s, pretrimmed paper, cut to strips slightly longer than the height of an average wall, eliminated some of the work of measuring and cutting. By 1953 Imperial Wallpaper's entire line was pretrimmed, prepasted, and "ready to wear." Its advertisements claimed: "Just wet and hang."[21] By making it easier for homeowners to hang wallpaper, these innovations helped make wallpaper manufacturers more competitive in the changing marketplace. One survey estimated that homeowners did sixty percent of the nation's paperhanging in the early 1950s.[22]

THE DEVELOPMENT OF NEW SYNTHETIC MATERIALS further increased the design possibilities for would-be remodelers and provided them

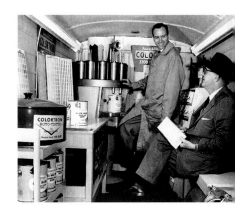

TOP A colorant-dispensing machine being demonstrated inside a manufacturer's display truck, ca. 1965. The "roto-tinter" in the left foreground was a less-expensive manual alternative to the big machine and merely contained cans of colorant and a ladle.

OPPOSITE PAGE Cover of "Color Perfect Wallpaper," 1945

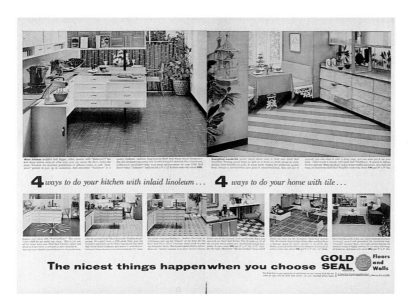

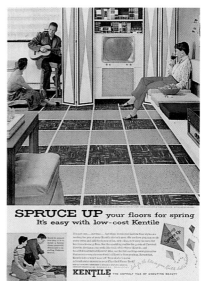

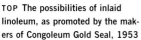

TOP The possibilities of inlaid
linoleum, as promoted by the makers of Congoleum Gold Seal, 1953

Asphalt tile was a commonly
used and inexpensive flooring
material, 1956.

BOTTOM Valspar paint advertisement, 1955

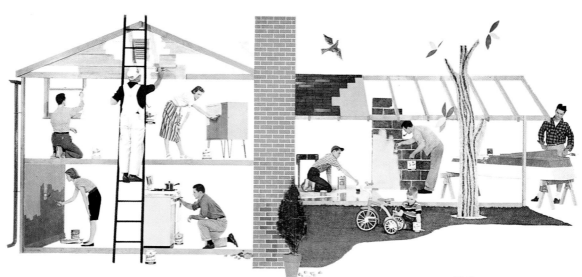

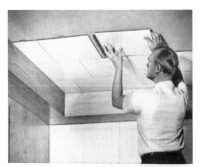

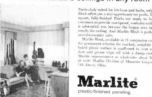

Advertisement for Marlite Block
as ceiling tile, 1961

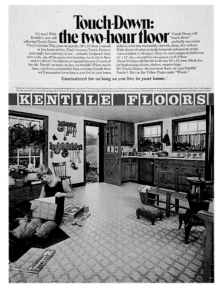

Self-adhesive tile apparently made
the installation of flooring so easy,
one could do it without moving
furniture or appliances, 1971.

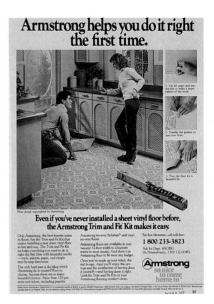

A couple using the Armstrong Trim
and Fit Kit, which contained sheet
vinyl flooring as well as installation
tools, instructions, and
pattern paper, 1984

with easier ways to decorate on their own. Companies used plastics to
manufacture a broad spectrum of decorative laminates, wall paneling,
and floor coverings.[23] In the 1950s, vinyl overtook linoleum as the
most popular floor covering. Originally available in large rolls requiring
special cutting tools and installation skills, both materials were
soon sold in standard-sized tiles or small squares. Within two decades,
vinyl tile was available with a self-adhesive back for easy installation.
Amateurs needed only ordinary hand tools to cover old walls with
lightweight panels such as Marlite, a masonite product with a
melamine plastic finish introduced by Marsh Wall Products, Inc.
Plastic decorative paneling was available in different colors and sizes,
as were prefinished hardwood panels, introduced by the U.S.
Plywood Corporation in the mid-1940s under the names Plankweld
and Weldtex.[24]

NOT ALL DESIRABLE DECORATIVE EFFECTS, however, could be
achieved with equal ease by amateur remodelers. Many of the plastic
paneling and flooring products required special tools and skills for
cutting and installation. Professional contractors and remodelers
remained in the picture, in part because many local building codes
required that only trained experts handle certain types of jobs.
Manufacturers and consumers alike understood the limits of do-it-
yourself marketing: producers continued to sell to members of the
building trades, and homeowners chose selectively which home-
improvement activities to undertake themselves.

Buying and Selling Do-It-Yourself

The customer more and more building supply houses are out to cultivate is none other than you—the week-end builder, amateur handyman, basement cabinetmaker.
JONATHAN ALEY, "SUPER MARKETS FOR THE AMATEUR HANDYMAN," *AMERICAN HOME*, AUGUST 1955[25]

EQUALLY IMPORTANT TO THE AMATEUR BUILDER or handyman was the transformation of the way home-improvement products were bought and sold after World War II. Because most repairs and remodeling projects had been executed by professional contractors in the years before 1940, hardware stores and lumberyards had catered primarily to these skilled men. Average consumers or would-be do-it-yourselfers found few retail outlets readily accessible to them. Many power tools, for example, were first available only by mail order. Lumberyards had traditionally served the building trades, offering discounts to commercial remodeling operations. They sold construction supplies in large quantities to customers who knew what they wanted and how to use the supplies they purchased. It took some time for retailers of building supplies to learn to accept and serve the "one-board customer."[26]

BEFORE THE WAR, consumers did have some options for purchasing home-improvement supplies. Mail-order catalogs were important sources of materials for repair and remodeling, particularly for rural families. Hardware stores had emerged in the 19th century, deriving their name from the "builder's hardware"—doorknobs, hinges, and tools—that they sold primarily to members of the building trades.[27] By the early 20th century, many hardware stores offered a wide range of merchandise including sporting goods, farm implements, cutlery, and kitchen utensils, as well as building supplies. Much like general stores, these hardware stores sold goods to whomever would buy.[28]

BEGINNING IN THE 1920S AND 1930S, hardware-store owners and managers gradually began catering to homeowners interested in making basic repairs and taking on remodeling projects.[29] The rising popularity of do-it-yourself in the 1950s encouraged many building-

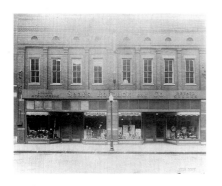

Exterior of the Sears retail store in Paducah, Kentucky, which opened in 1928

Fred P. Johnson's Gibson City, Illinois hardware store, 1924. Typical of independent hardware retailers before World War II, this 25-by-113-foot store employed three people: Mr. Johnson (left); his son, Russ (right); and Harvey Murry, a harness repairman (center). A customer is in the background.

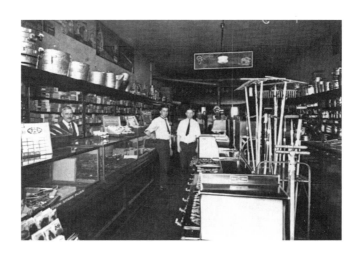

supply retailers to redesign their stores to specifically target amateur handymen and women as their primary customers. To bring themselves up to date with other contemporary shopping environments, they incorporated self-service merchandising techniques pioneered in supermarkets. Early hardware stores had kept most goods in bulk containers behind the counter. Store layouts and operations required the assistance of a salesperson not only in making choices but also in inspecting the goods for sale. In self-service displays, shoppers could see and handle prepackaged goods arranged on open counters. To attract new consumers and encourage them to stay in the store longer, hardware stores sought to glamorize their displays and to showcase an enlarged stock of building materials and equipment. Stores were designed to be large and spacious, to facilitate shopping and browsing for a wider clientele and to accommodate rushes of weekend customers in a short period of time. Larger stores divided their displays by intended use into departments or sections. Central Hardware Company in St. Louis, Missouri, for example, created a "modernization" department where model kitchens, refrigerators, stoves, and other large appliances were displayed.[30]

FAR BOTTOM Levittown Hardware, Levittown, New York, 1951

BOTTOM The departmentalized and uncluttered look of a self-service Ace store in Minneapolis, Minnesota, ca. 1960

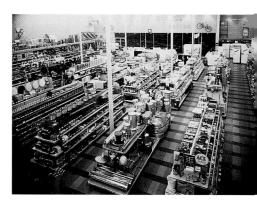

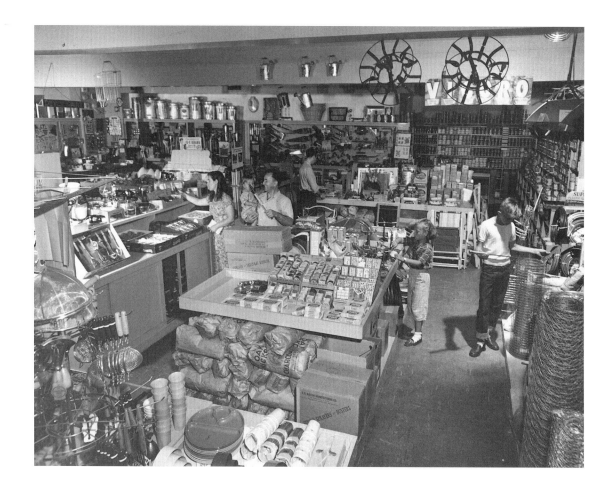

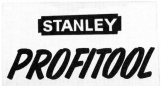

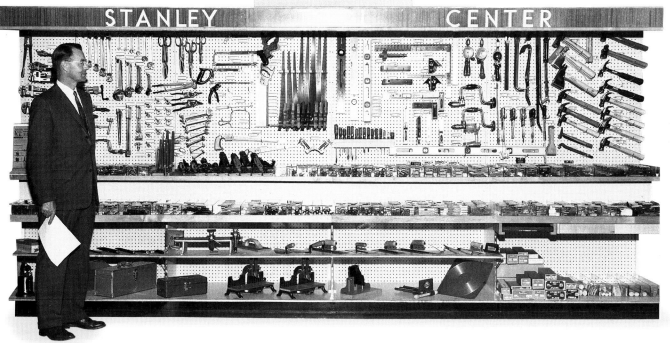

TOP The Stanley Profitool system exemplified the type of in-store product display that manufacturers designed for retailers, 1956.

BOTTOM This in-store display sold vinyl piping by offering plumbing instruction to do-it-yourselfers, ca. 1980.

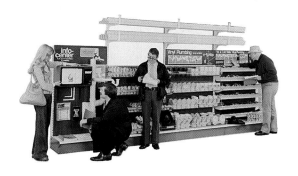

RETAILERS LEARNED ABOUT WAYS to use these new merchandising techniques to broaden their customer base from trade publications such as *Hardware Retailer*, *Hardware Age*, and *Hardware Merchandiser*. As well, they increasingly turned to industry groups such as the American Hardware Manufacturers Association, the National Retail Hardware Association, and the National Lumber Dealers Association for support in selling to do-it-yourself customers. MANUFACTURERS WORKED WITH HARDWARE-STORE MANAGERS to ensure that their products were prominently and appealingly presented and within easy reach of potential shoppers. Their marketing departments developed display units, or "merchandisers," that showcased power tools, building materials, and decorating supplies in an inviting manner. For example, the Stanley Works created the Profitool system to display its line of hand tools for amateurs. Items such as nails, screws, and drill bits were prepackaged in convenient quantities and hung on racks within customers' reach.[31] These packages improved the saleability of products by incorporating features such as clear plastic casing, colorful graphics, and simplified installation instructions. HARDWARE STORES ADVERTISED THEMSELVES as service centers for would-be amateur remodelers in need of advice as well as supplies. To project this identity, many stores incorporated the do-it-yourself idea into their names. Posted on large signs along the suburban roadside, store names such as "Home Supply Center," "Do-It-Yourself Headquarters," and "Home Handyman Center" beckoned homeowners

into expanded parking lots. These stores commonly established evening hours so homeowners could shop after work. Many of them also added to their sales techniques an educational dimension, welcoming novices as well as experienced handymen. Customers found not only the supplies they needed for home-improvement projects but also helpful guidance, and sometimes free printed brochures, about how to approach a given project. The Huntington Materials Corporation in Huntington, New York, for example, established an "Instruct-O-Matic Home Remodelers Clinic" every Thursday night.[32] Like other hardware retail outlets, lumberyards also employed many of the same mass-merchandising techniques.[33]

AS A CONSUMER MARKET for home-improvement supplies developed and expanded, chain stores and discounters championed mass-merchandising techniques most effectively. They moved into the do-it-yourself market with high-demand goods such as power tools and small appliances. To compete better with these "mass merchandisers," independent hardware and lumber dealers joined together to form hardware wholesale companies. To strengthen their buying power, twenty-five small retailers chartered in 1948 a wholesale buying cooperative called Cotter & Co., which became known by the True Value Stores it established. Similar business organizations such as Ace Hardware and Hardware Wholesalers, Inc. took off in the postwar decades.[34]

BY 1970, INDEPENDENT HARDWARE STORES and old-line chains such as Sears and Montgomery Ward's began to face competition from a new kind of retailer: the home center. The managers of these stores explicitly designed their displays and marketing campaigns for the do-it-yourselfer rather than the professional builder.[35] Home centers were bigger than hardware stores and had a much wider selection of merchandise. Whereas most hardware stores stocked less than

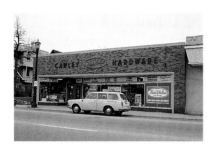

Cawley Hardware, a store belonging to Cotter & Co.'s True Value cooperative, 1976

BOTTOM Educational image used in a late-1950s campaign by the National Lumber Dealers Association to instruct lumber and hardware retailers on modern store design and sales techniques, ca. 1960

BOTTOM RIGHT National Lumber Dealers Association educational photo, ca. 1960

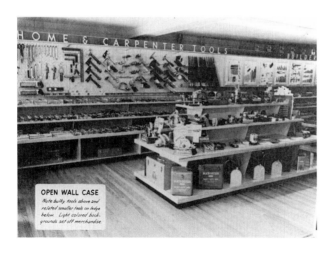

OPEN WALL CASE
Note bulky tools above and related smaller tools on ledge below. Light colored backgrounds set off merchandise.

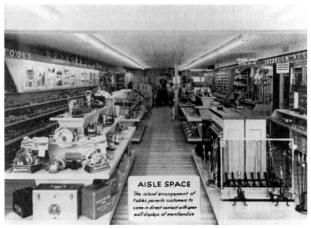

AISLE SPACE
The island arrangement of tables permits customers to come in direct contact with open wall displays of merchandise.

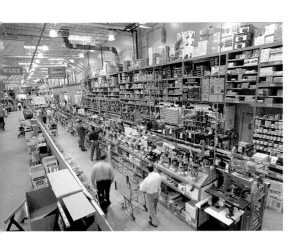

The indoor sales floor of the average Home Depot warehouse-style hardware store covers 105,000 square feet, 1996.

twelve thousand items in the early 1980s, home centers such as Lowe's, Payless Cashways, and Hechinger's kept forty thousand or more items on the shelves.[36] By offering many different types of products under one roof, these stores provided one-stop shopping, eliminating the need for separate visits to the paint store, nursery, and lumberyard. Home centers attempted to provide shoppers with the security of knowing what was available and aimed to ensure that products would be in stock.

BY THE LATE 1970S, consumer research found that about seventy-five percent of all American households were involved in some type of do-it-yourself activity. Yet the number of do-it-yourselfers entering the market was slowing.[37] As the market approached saturation, hardware stores, home centers, lumberyards, and other retail establishments selling home-improvement products competed intensely for the consumer's dollar.

PRICE COMPETITION LED SOME RETAILERS to take the home-center concept a step further. In 1979 Home Depot opened its first store in Atlanta, Georgia, and introduced the idea of a home-improvement retail warehouse. Home Depot's huge, multiacre stores purchased stock in such large quantities that on many items it could offer consumers exceptionally low prices. By stacking merchandise to the ceilings in wide shopping aisles, Home Depot's store layout further encouraged a low-price image. Do-it-yourselfers responded positively with increased purchases. By 1997, there were more than five hundred Home Depot stores throughout the United States.[38]

THE POWER AND SUCCESS of Home Depot's business strategy has had a dramatic impact on the buying and selling of home-improvement supplies in the 1990s. The older home centers have adopted many of Home Depot's warehouse techniques. Less efficient, small independent and mid-sized chain retailers have had trouble competing, and many of them have gone out of business. Many of today's smaller stores rely on an affiliation with wholesale buying cooperatives for support. Discounting and warehouse-retailing have meant lower prices and more choices for consumers, but also more confusion about what to buy and where to buy it.[39]

ALTHOUGH UNPRECEDENTED NUMBERS OF MARRIED WOMEN continued to enter the paid labor force after the war, middle-class women were expected to stay at home and raise families.[7] As women saw the pieces of this new domestic life coming together, many discovered home improvement as a purposeful alternative to working outside the home. By planning and completing repair and remodeling projects, they enhanced their role as homemakers. Families who were first-time homeowners especially had much to learn about the era's new household "necessities." By mastering these challenges, women could earn status and recognition from their husbands, children, and neighbors. In this sense, many women drew on their stereotypical position as domestic guardians to derive power and influence through a focus on home improvement.

MANY WOMEN CONTINUED to assume responsibility for home repair in peacetime, but not all had the necessary skills. Frustration with their limitations led two homemakers to establish a home-repair school for women in 1950. Grace K. Liebman had flown for the Civil Air Patrol spotting submarines and had worked for the Army's interceptor command. Lillian Baldwin had served with the Office of Strategic Services in Europe. When the two women became friends in New York City after the war, they searched for a place to learn how "to cope with everyday home problems." Finding only specialized industrial-arts classes, Liebman and Baldwin established the Know-How Workshop in midtown Manhattan. The school offered short courses for generalists, led by licensed shop teachers who trained

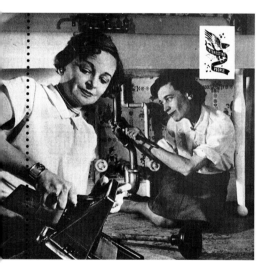

TOP Lillian Baldwin and Grace Liebman, the founders of the Know-How Workshop, featured in *The American Magazine*, 1950

RIGHT Hotpoint designed these plastic appliance models to aid kitchen planning and took it for granted that women played the leading role in that activity, 1948.

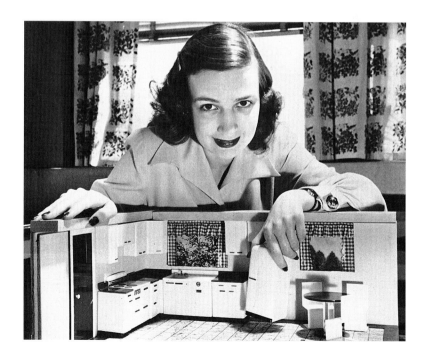

Madame, when it comes to home decoration, you are the chief executive! By a mere wave of your hand, you can summon all the gay, glorious colors of nature and bring fresh beauty into dull, lifeless rooms.
PITTSBURGH PAINTS ADVERTISEMENT, 1939[4]

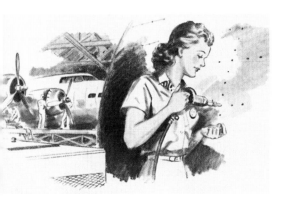

Women worked in most areas of industry during World War II, including in aircraft assembly plants, 1942.

THE EXPERIENCES OF WORLD WAR II forced many women to reevaluate their place in the home. The shortage of male labor during wartime had created new opportunities for women in the workplace, and these work experiences had provided women with new technical abilities. As war workers in the defense industry, they had learned to operate heavy machinery such as rivet guns, metal lathes, and drill presses. Women had also used their newfound skills and confidence to take charge of home maintenance and repair while men were away at war and skilled repairmen were in short supply.[5]

HOME-IMPROVEMENT LITERATURE of the wartime era had reflected this new reality. *House & Garden's Wartime Manual for the Home* (1943) included carpentry, electrical wiring, and plumbing among the "home repairs any woman can make"; a separate section categorized most structural repairs to walls, doors, and windows as tasks for men. *House Beautiful* published a similar manual which provided house-maintenance tips through a homemaker-friendly format of recipe cards. These recipes gave instructions on everything from patching a plaster wall to laying linoleum flooring to repairing a hole in a window screen. Women used this kind of advice to "make it do" until the war's end.[6]

House Beautiful's wartime maintenance manuals provided advice about home repairs and frequently assumed that women would be doing the work, 1944.

LINOLEUM

How To Lay Linoleum

To lay a linoleum floor, you'll need a hammer, linoleum knife, sandbags, ruler, pencil, scissors, thumbtacks, heavy cardboard, paste spreader, and linoleum cement. If laid over wood, surface must be smooth and all nails hammered down. If floor was painted or varnished, remove old finish. Sand or plane down uneven floors. Fill cracks with wood filler. Linoleum can be laid over old linoleum if there are no breaks, and old wax is removed. For illustrated instructions, send 25¢ to Paraffine Companies, San Francisco, for "Home Owner's Primer for Laying Linoleum."

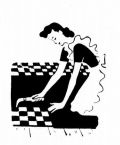

OVER ☞

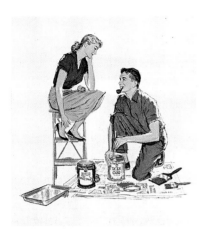

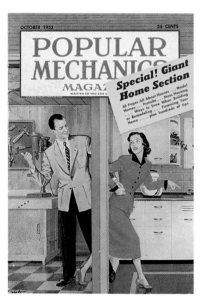

FAR TOP Selling paint by evoking dreams of domestic bliss, from a Sherwin-Williams advertisement, 1957

TOP Cover of *Popular Mechanics*, October 1953

PRODUCT ADVERTISEMENTS AND MAGAZINE ARTICLES from this era provide evidence of the messages about gender that men and women encountered as they shopped for remodeling products and services, and made decisions about what home-improvement projects to initiate, how they should be done, and who should do them. Advertising images generally present oversimplified versions of real life, embodying assumptions about consumers in the effort to sell products. Most advertisers of do-it-yourself products defined married couples and nuclear families as their primary market. Popular magazines also located do-it-yourself home improvement in the context of married family life. Advertisements and advice literature implied that first came marriage, then came do-it-yourself home improvement, and many commercial representations equated do-it-yourself with domestic bliss. Archetypal husbands and wives, often with a young son (rarely a daughter), were shown happily working on projects together. The implied family harmony prompted one commentator to suggest that "do it yourself" be called "do it together."[3]

AT THE SAME TIME, advertising differentiated the abilities and roles of men and women, and worked hard to make traditional gender divisions seem natural. Women may have completed projects in home workshops while their husbands fixed dinner, but you would not have known it from the ads! Advertisements usually assigned women and men stereotypical roles, and often pictured husbands and wives working in separate household spaces. For example, a 1953 *Popular Mechanics* cover depicted a woman darting into her kitchen and a man heading into a home workshop. And when a married couple joined forces to paint a house on the cover of a 1958 Sherwin-Williams booklet, the husband took the rougher job of exterior painting on a ladder, while the wife remained inside to make the place homey with the help of an easy-to-use paint roller.

A CLOSE EXAMINATION OF THE MEDIA of the postwar period reveals not only the rigid notions of different male and female interests and abilities that were common to postwar America, but also widespread confusion about the appropriate roles for men and women. Advertisements for tools, decorative supplies, and other remodeling equipment suggest that manufacturers, designers, retailers, and advertisers were often uncertain about which spouse made home-improvement decisions, and whether men or women would carry out the projects.

Handyman, Handywoman

House building is essentially a masculine function. The man contributes the material element, he uses his knowledge; and the result is an agglomeration of wood and stone. The house is built, and it's a good house; and then comes along the woman, and with her feeling, her sentiment, her intuition, she transforms the house into a home.
"HOUSE BUILDING AND HOME MAKING," *THE HOUSE BEAUTIFUL*, SEPTEMBER 1915 [1]

The expanding do-it-yourself marketplace became an arena for Americans to work out complex and changing ideas about male and female identity in relation to the postwar home. After the depression and four years of war, both women and men faced confusing new circumstances as they sought to fulfill their long-delayed dreams of home and family. During the war, women had been given new career opportunities, and many had taken sole charge of their households in their husbands' absence. As families sought to realize the ideal of suburban living in the postwar period, they reinvented a central role for women in the home. At the same time, the men returning home looked to reestablish themselves in the domestic sphere, and tried to meet shifting expectations that they could act as both providers and nurturers.[2]

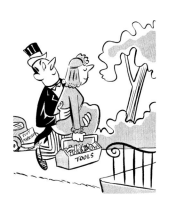

This cartoon by Morris Brickman pointed out the most commom assumption behind the idea of do-it-yourself home improvement: that "homeowner" meant "married couple," 1955.

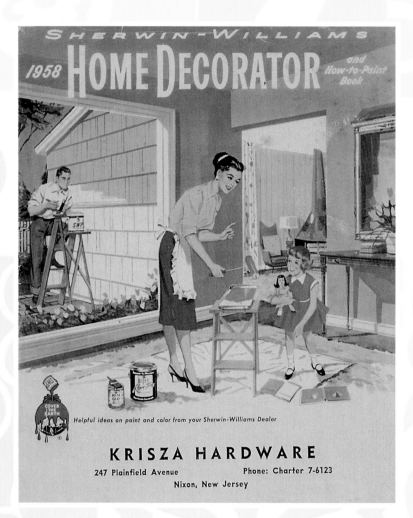

TOP The nuclear family at home, each member painting according to stereotypical divisions of labor and household space, from Sherwin-Williams's *1958 Home Decorator and How-to-Paint Book*

PREVIOUS PAGE A couple converting storage space into a spare bedroom, 1954

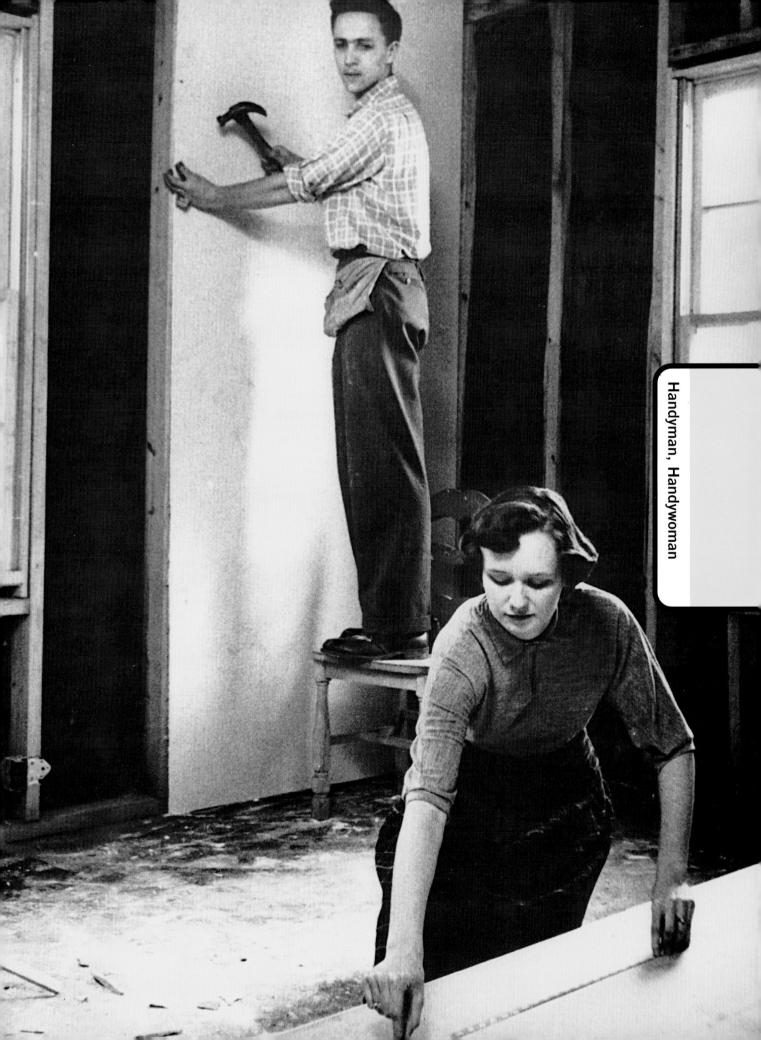

Handyman, Handywoman

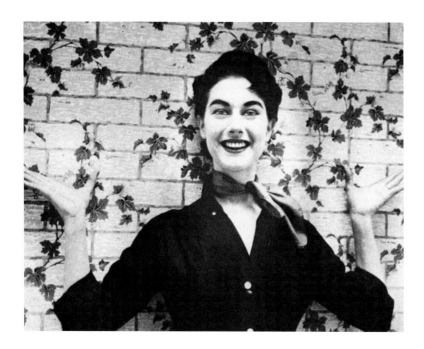

students to patch cracks in plaster walls, repair leaky faucets and clogged drains, and replace sash cords in broken windows. This school provided at least some women with technical skills that had been normally taught only to boys.[8]

BY THE EARLY 1950S, a survey showed that women not only initiated more home-improvement projects than men, but actually took on more of the "muscle work."[9] Recognizing the growing importance of women as consumers of their products, home-improvement advertisers and publishers began to change their marketing strategies. Representations of homemakers often showed them initiating remodeling projects, devising strategies for executing them, and directing the rest of the family toward realizing plans. The female connection with home planning became solidified in the 1950s and 1960s, when humorists commonly depicted women as the brains and inspiration behind do-it-yourself projects. But confusion over which projects women would want to undertake still reigned.

ADVERTISEMENTS PORTRAYED INTERIOR DECORATING as a quintessentially female activity. Long considered part of a woman's homemaking duties, subjects such as color selection, furnishing, and the design of wall and window treatments were regularly taught in home-economics courses for girls and young women. Advertisements for decorating products targeted women almost exclusively and depicted them dreamily envisioning an ideal wallpaper or floor-tile pattern. A 1940s Luminall paint brochure, for example, suggested that women possessed the innate aesthetic ability — or even magical power! — required to properly choose paint colors.

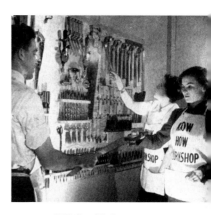

TOP LEFT With the aid of easy-to-hang and easy-to-maintain Wall-Tex, this woman seems to have achieved both home beauty and personal happiness, 1956.

TOP Women learned the basics of hand-tool use in preparation for undertaking their own home repairs at the Know-How Workshop, 1950.

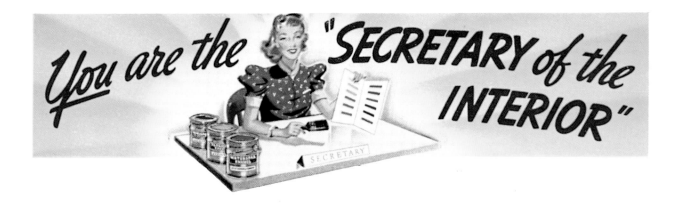

ADVERTISEMENTS AND INSTRUCTIONAL LITERATURE often classified
building as outside the realm of women's responsibility. *Better Homes
and Gardens* published separate home-improvement manuals for men
and women: the *Better Homes and Gardens Handyman's Book* (1951)
addressed male readers, while its companion *Decorator's Book* was
clearly intended for a female audience. Since the early 20th century,
advertisements had shown women performing only a limited set
of home repair or remodeling tasks. Again and again, women appeared
refinishing floors, painting window trim, polishing furniture, or
doing other small projects — but never actually constructing things.
In assuming responsibility for maintaining the condition of the home's
surfaces, the ideal homemaker literally seemed to take charge of her
family's refinement. Detailed attention to surface treatments, many
advertisements implied, stemmed from women's socially prescribed
obligation to safeguard the cleanliness of the home.[10] When electric
power tools for amateurs were introduced in the 1940s, magazines
and advertisements drew on this convention and showed women using
them only in certain circumscribed situations — to polish or buff various surfaces, for instance. A 1954 *Popular Science* article suggested
that women could use a drill in the kitchen to polish silver, scour pots,
or even mix milkshakes.[11]

BUT, AS DO-IT-YOURSELF MARKETING EXPANDED in the 1950s and
1960s and manufacturers began to promote a wider range of products, women's growing involvement with remodeling tasks became
reflected more in advertisements, trade literature, and other popular
media. By suggesting that "even a woman could do it," advertisements sometimes suggested that a given home-improvement task was
easy. Women at first appeared only as assistants to their husbands in
technical matters. Typically, women were assigned roles requiring less
skill; with remarkable consistency, the men even appeared much taller
than the women in these images. For example, in a Marlite ceiling tile
brochure, a man stands on a ladder installing tile in a kitchen.

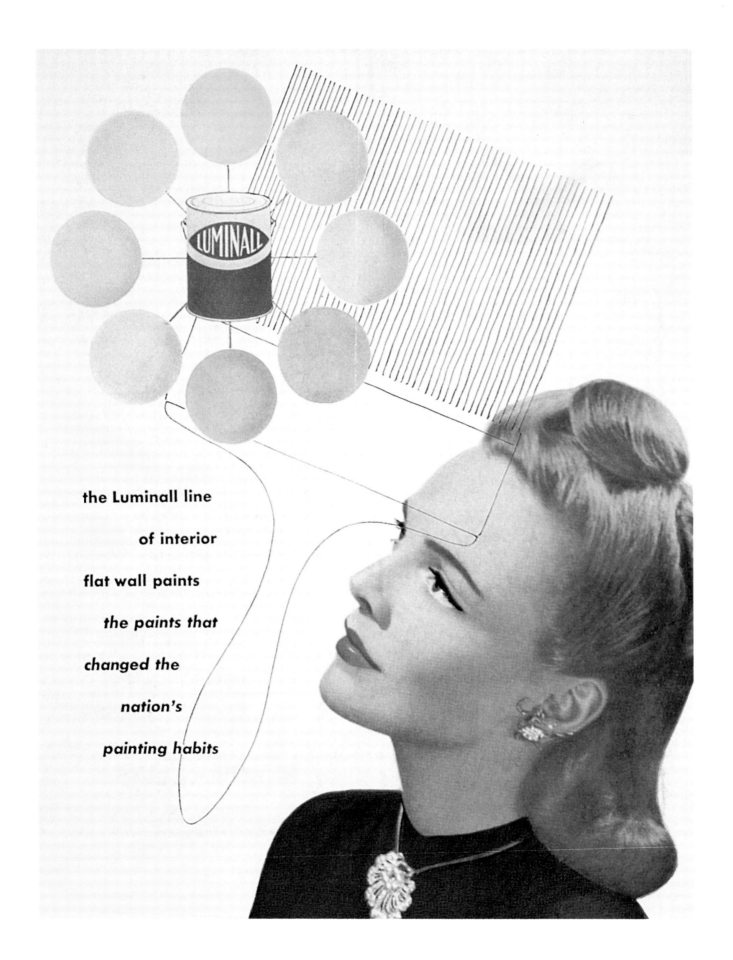

the Luminall line

of interior

flat wall paints

the paints that

changed the

nation's

painting habits

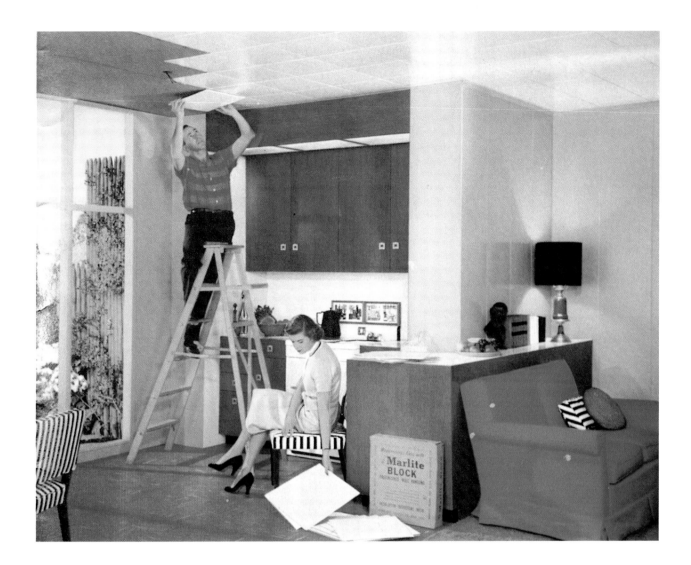

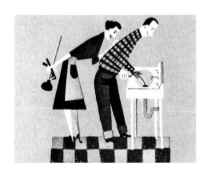

FAR TOP Couple paneling a room, from a Marlite Plank and Block brochure, 1958

TOP Drawing from the *Better Homes and Gardens Handyman's Book*, 1951

A woman assists by handing him tiles from out of a box on the floor — a common scenario. He works with the product, while she removes it from the container.

IN SPITE OF WOMEN'S CENTRAL AND DIVERSE ROLES in do-it-yourself home improvement in the 1950s and 1960s, advertisements and magazines stopped short of portraying them as fully capable in technical areas. Depictions of female do-it-yourselfers in advertisements and popular literature reflected the era's ambivalence about women's employment and their expanded participation in home improvement. Most magazines acknowledged women's power and responsibility in the planning and decorative realms, but were less clear about how women shared responsibility with their husbands when it came to the physical rebuilding of the postwar home.

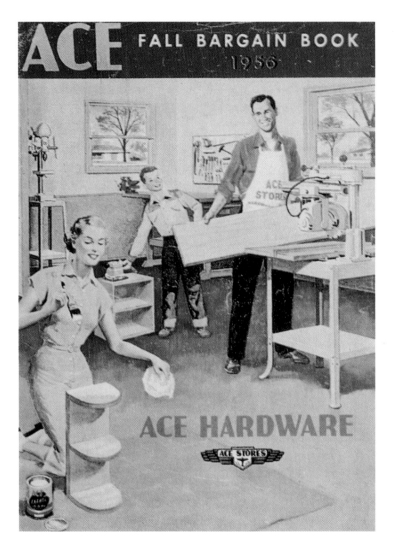

ACE FALL BARGAIN BOOK 1956

ACE HARDWARE

ACE STORES

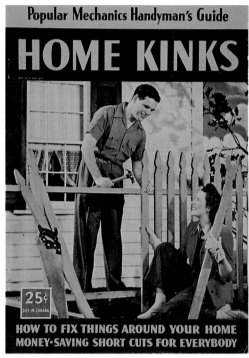

Popular Mechanics Handyman's Guide

HOME KINKS

25¢
30¢ IN CANADA

HOW TO FIX THINGS AROUND YOUR HOME
MONEY-SAVING SHORT CUTS FOR EVERYBODY

Look what you can do with

A Drill in the Kitchen

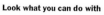

MOUNTED UNDER CABINET near sink, ¼" electric drill with buffer wheel will put a high shine on silver, chrome and copper ware. Fitted with wire cup brush, it also makes short work of pot-scouring chores. Use can-opener bracket to hold drill, as for wall clip below, but add spring cupboard latch (inset at right) to lock drill so it can't slide out.

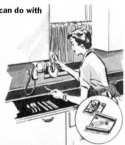

¼" DIA.
ROD OR
SMALLER

CAN-OPENER BRACKET makes simple slip-in clip to hold drill on wall. Bracket is mounted on 1½"-thick wood block so mixer blade will clear wall. Metal plate on drill is hacksawed to shape of bracket from heavy sheet (cover plate from old electrical junction box is just right). Plate is then slotted and strapped on with large truck-type hose clamp.

COOL SUMMER MILK SHAKES are mixed in a jiffy with drill mounted on kitchen wall this way. Drill can also be used as hand mixer for beating eggs and batters in large bowls. Beater can be short rod bent at tip or small commercial impeller available at hardware stores.

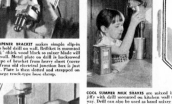

KNIFE SHARPENER puts a quick, keen edge on knives without hand grinding. Sharpener, made by Mall Tool Co., fits ¼" chucks, has a groove that you just slip knife into.

CLOCKWISE FROM TOP LEFT

In the do-it-yourself family conceived by many advertisers, the husband built things, usually with the aid of power tools, and the wife took care of surfaces. Cover of the *Ace Fall Bargain Book*, 1956.

According to many media portrayals, a woman's technical role in home improvement involved helping her husband. Cover of *Home Kinks*, the *Popular Mechanics* handyman's guide, 1943.

Advertisers and magazines typically showed women using power tools for cleaning or polishing, rarely for construction or repair, as in this *Popular Science* article, 1954.

Driving nails is work—no doubt about it. But it's also the kind of clean, thumping exercise a man can enjoy. There's smacking satisfaction in belting a shiny tenpenny into stout 2 x 4 studding....Hammers up, men.
STANLEY TOOLS ADVERTISEMENT, *POPULAR MECHANICS*, OCTOBER 1956[12]

MEN ENTERED THE POSTWAR HOME seeking to be simultaneously masculine and domestic. Many couples had never owned a home—and neither had their parents. Economic prosperity provided young men with stable salaries, including paid vacations, as well as a new array of things to buy for the home—a more bewildering cornucopia of consumer goods than ever before. Families relied on husbands and fathers to provide income with which to purchase appliances, cars, and toys, but also expected Dad to "pitch in" with the domestic routine.

IN RESPONDING TO THESE EXPECTATIONS IN THE 1950S, men tried to establish a place for themselves in suburban domestic life in ways that conformed to earlier notions of masculinity involving technology and industry. The association of tools with masculinity was rooted in the predominance of male workers in 19th-century centers of production, especially in heavy industry, as well as in the previous century's pervasive idea that men and women belonged in separate public and private spheres respectively. In the early 20th century, many middle-class men took up woodworking hobbies, in part because manual work seemed to offer a connection to masculinity that was absent in the white-collar work routines of modern urban society.[13] It also helped men to distinguish themselves from the female world of consumption.

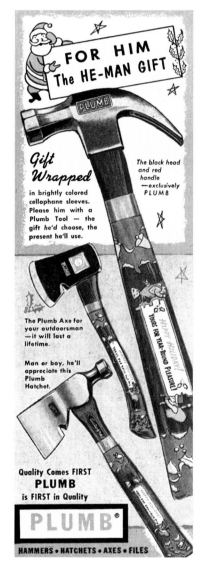

TOP Advertisement for Plumb tools, 1952

RIGHT The tools of industry, construction, and repair traditionally had strongly masculine associations, 1943.

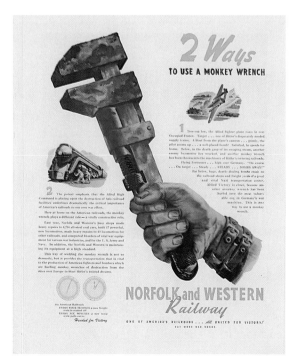

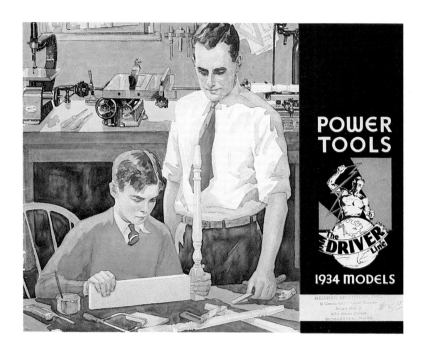

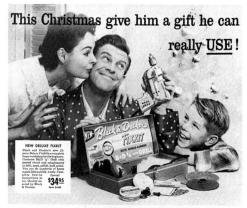

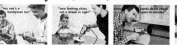

AS THE INTEREST IN DO-IT-YOURSELF HOME IMPROVEMENT gained momentum in the 1950s, increasing numbers of men created male spheres inside their homes by establishing home workshops in basements or garages. As historian Steven Gelber has explained: "This new masculine space permitted men to be both a part of the house and apart from it, sharing the home with their families while retaining roles that suburban men created so that they could actively participate in family activities while retaining spatial and functional autonomy."[14] And because what men did around the house had economic value, these projects carried the legitimacy of masculine skilled labor. Home repair, which had begun as leisure activity— not housework—became a central focus of men's suburban lives. Through do-it-yourself home improvement, many men achieved what Steven Gelber has called "domestic masculinity."[15]

ADVERTISEMENTS FOR TOOLS, especially power tools, tapped into male homeowners' desires to participate in domestic life while also retaining a certain type of masculine identity. On the one hand, power-tool manufacturers promoted their products as suitable for use in the home. On the other hand, their marketing campaigns rein-forced the message that men, unlike women, were naturally suited to building. Power-tool advertisements cast the equation of mascu-linity with technological expertise in 20th-century terms by addressing their potential consumers as "handymen." Whereas "handyman" had once referred to a hired hand, it now described the homeowning amateur, and implied that do-it-yourselfers were men.

TOP What better way for the man of the house to achieve his home improvement goals than for his wife to give him a drill and its accessories? 1956

TOP LEFT Father and son engaged in a carpentry project, from a Walker-Turner Co. power tools trade catalog, 1934

ADVERTISEMENTS FOR HAND TOOLS AND POWER TOOLS for home use often pictured older and younger men together. Such images made romanticized references to preindustrial workplaces, where technical skills were passed from generation to generation by way of an apprenticeship system. By the late 1950s, several campaigns showcased Hollywood movie stars such as Ricardo Montalban using power tools with their sons.[16] Such ads framed home improvement as a family activity where the father/son relationship was key.

OTHER MARKETING CAMPAIGNS attempted to define hammers, axes, and saws as quintessential "man gifts" or, more emphatically, "he-man gifts." Drawing on the assumption that tools made men happy, advertisements invited women and children to give tools to Dad on Father's Day or at Christmas. Specially packaged holiday toolboxes helped establish home-workshop equipment as the proper present for a woman to give to her husband. Popular humor identified a love of tools as a particularly male obsession.

DO-IT-YOURSELF HOME IMPROVEMENT was also presented as a man's domestic duty. *American Magazine* reported on a wedding shower for midwestern bachelor Dick Wilson at which his friends gave him a hammer, saw, pliers, electric drill, and a lawn mower. The groom-to-be and his intended planned to settle in a trailer in Huntington, Indiana, on a lot where they hoped to build a ranch house one day. With tools purchased from a hardware store, Dick's friends and family equipped him "to become the handy husband personified."[17]

WOMEN GIVING TOOLS TO THEIR HUSBANDS conveyed specific assumptions about the man's role in the household. Many women expected men to apply their abilities with tools and carpentry to make home improvements rather than just to pursue a hobby. Being a good family man required being handy and undertaking projects for women, as implied in a 1952–53 *Family Handyman* cover showing a man proudly presenting a completed kitchen project to his wife. If a husband did not make regular repairs and improvements to the family home, some media representations even went so far as to suggest that he was lazy and incompetent.

BUT MEN DID NOT NECESSARILY KNOW how to perform all of the various home-improvement tasks expected of them. Not all of them had learned about household repair and woodworking from their fathers. Eager to please and rise to familial expectations, many men welcomed do-it-yourself products that placed ambitious home-improvement goals within their grasp. More than ever before, amateur handymen relied on tips from neighbors, hardware-store salesmen, and especially instruction manuals and how-to magazines. With the help of these publications, men learned how to be good husbands, just as cookbooks of the era spelled out a wife's domestic duties.

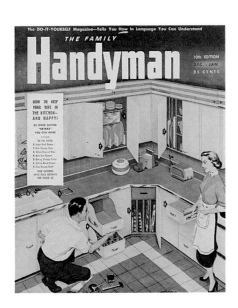

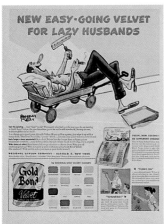

FAR TOP Cover of *The Family Handyman*, December-January 1952–53

TOP Husbands who were not handy or did not enjoy home improvement risked being labeled as lazy, as suggested by this Gold Bond Velvet paint advertisement, 1953.

HROUGH THE 1960S, many advertisements for power tools targeted a male clientele to the extent that they obscured the importance of women in do-it-yourself home-improvement as planners, designers, and, in fact, builders. In the early 1970s, feminist critics began to protest gender stereotypes in the media. Citing contradictions between the realities of women's lives and the ways they were represented in print and on television, they forced magazine editors and advertisers to reexamine women's place in American society—and their identity as consumers. In response to these changes, and sensing an untapped market, manufacturers and retailers of do-it-yourself home-repair and decorating equipment began to market a broader array of products to women.

NEW KINDS OF INSTRUCTION MANUALS APPEARED on the market, aimed specifically at female do-it-yourselfers. These books challenged the "handyman" myth and were based on the assumption that women could be every bit as handy as men. In *I Took A Hammer in My Hand: The Woman's Build-It and Fix-It Handbook* (1973), Florence Adams sought to contribute to a literature "for the handy*person*, women and men doing tasks, women no longer the helper but the doer."[19] Books like hers demonstrated that repairs were easier than they appeared, and gave women the know-how and confidence to solve many household problems. The feminine how-to genre

For all the cultural dogma that puts a doll carriage under the Christmas tree for a girl when a pair of pliers might be better, the real repairman in the average household is, by default, that girl, now grown, after twenty years of careful protection from anything resembling a tool.
JAMES L. A. WEBB AND BARTON L. HOUSEMAN, *THE YOU-DON'T-NEED-A-MAN-TO-FIX-IT BOOK: THE WOMAN'S GUIDE TO CONFIDENT HOME REPAIR*, 1973 [18]

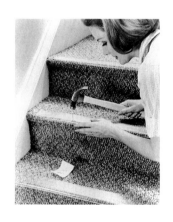

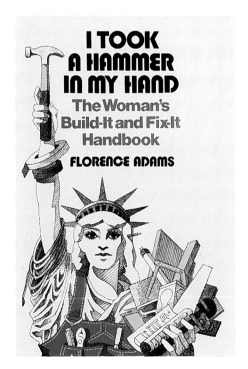

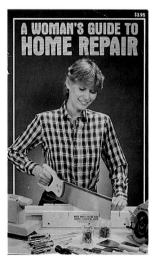

TOP Woman using a hammer to install transparent carpet edging, 1964

FAR LEFT By depicting Lady Liberty triumphantly wielding home-improvement tools, artist and author Florence Adams challenged the myth of the handyman in her cover illustration for *I Took a Hammer in My Hand*, 1973.

LEFT Cover of *A Woman's Guide to Home Repair*, 1979

IN ADDITION TO FURNITURE AND CABINETRY, IT'S ALSO QUITE GOOD AT BUILDING REPUTATIONS.

THE CRAFTSMAN PLUNGE ROUTER. IT HAS A 3 1/2 HP SOFT-START MOTOR TO

ELIMINATE JUMPING. INFINITE DEPTH SETTINGS. ELECTRONIC SPEED CONTROL TO

ADJUST TO WOOD HARDNESS. AND HANDLE-MOUNTED FINGERTIP CONTROLS. ADD

TO THAT A SELECTION OF OVER 200 DIFFERENT ROUTER BITS AND ACCESSORIES

AND YOU WON'T JUST BE WORKING WOOD, YOU'LL BE WORKING MIRACLES.

CRAFTSMAN

EXCLUSIVELY AT SEARS AND SEARS HARDWARE STORES

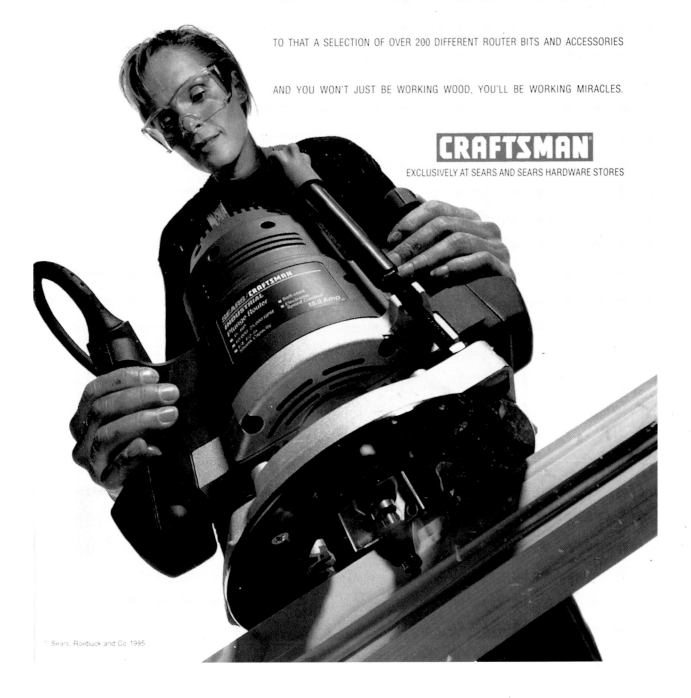

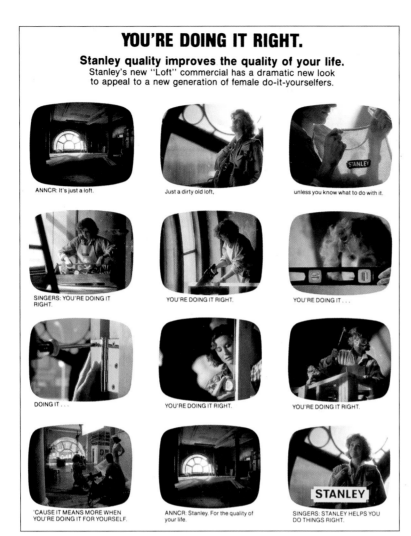

YOU'RE DOING IT RIGHT.

Stanley quality improves the quality of your life.
Stanley's new "Loft" commercial has a dramatic new look
to appeal to a new generation of female do-it-yourselfers.

ANNCR: It's just a loft.

Just a dirty old loft,

unless you know what to do with it.

SINGERS: YOU'RE DOING IT RIGHT.

YOU'RE DOING IT RIGHT.

YOU'RE DOING IT . . .

DOING IT . . .

YOU'RE DOING IT RIGHT.

YOU'RE DOING IT RIGHT.

'CAUSE IT MEANS MORE WHEN YOU'RE DOING IT FOR YOURSELF.

ANNCR: Stanley. For the quality of your life.

SINGERS: STANLEY HELPS YOU DO THINGS RIGHT.

STANLEY

LEFT **Without any assistance, a woman converted a loft into a photographic studio in the first Stanley television advertisement aimed solely at women, 1986.**

OPPOSITE PAGE **A women using a Craftsman industrial plunge router in a 1997 Sears advertisement**

responded in part to women's disappointment that few men lived up to their expectations as repairmen. *The You-Don't-Need-A-Man-To-Fix-It Book: The Woman's Guide to Confident Home Repair* (1973) estimated that "about four out of five men seem to be washouts as home repairers."[20]

THE NEWLY EMERGING HOME CENTERS OF THE 1970S similarly welcomed women into the realm of do-it-yourself home improvement. As one writer in *House Beautiful* pointed out, the carefully designed layout and liberal use of lighting in most home centers made them particularly accessible to women who might be frightened away from a more male-centered place. Many home centers also employed saleswomen to help their women customers feel more comfortable.[21] The success of home centers with women led lumberyard and hardware-store managers to take women's buying power more seriously than ever before. An industry survey of seven hundred women in the early 1980s found that more than half did their own painting,

wallpapering, carpentry, plastering, minor plumbing repairs, electrical
and appliance repair, upholstering, and gardening. Retailers attempted
to capitalize on this trend with a variety of new merchandising techniques designed to make shopping for home-improvement supplies
more appealing to women.[22]

WHEN CHANNEL HOME CENTERS NOTICED that almost half of their
customers were women, the chain hired women to help them develop
home-improvement clinics, booklets, and a free hotline for do-it-
yourselfers. Lowe's, which had previously catered to small contractors,
turned to its female customers in the early 1980s, when the number
of building starts declined. The company replaced warehouse-looking
stores with layouts resembling supermarkets, featuring wide, clearly
marked shopping aisles. Instead of displaying separate plumbing
fixtures, the store created complete model bathrooms. Lowe's also
added home-decorating products. As a result, Lowe's saw earnings
jump by forty-eight percent in the first quarter of 1982, proof
of women's buying power.[23]

REPRESENTATIONS OF WOMEN USING TOOLS — even power tools —
also became common in product advertisements in the 1980s.
Increasing numbers of marketing campaigns began showing women
remodeling on their own. An early example is the first Stanley
Tool advertisement that showed a woman completing a do-it-yourself
project without any help. The 1986 television commercial featured
a woman using Stanley products to convert a loft into a photography
studio. "You're doing it right," the commercial reassured women viewers.

CHANGES IN THE REPRESENTATIONS OF MEN AND WOMEN in
home-improvement magazines and advertisements reflected and
reinforced the transformation of the home in postwar America.
As gender roles shifted, manufacturers and retailers sought to promote
do-it-yourself products in ways that conformed to contemporary
notions of male and female identity.

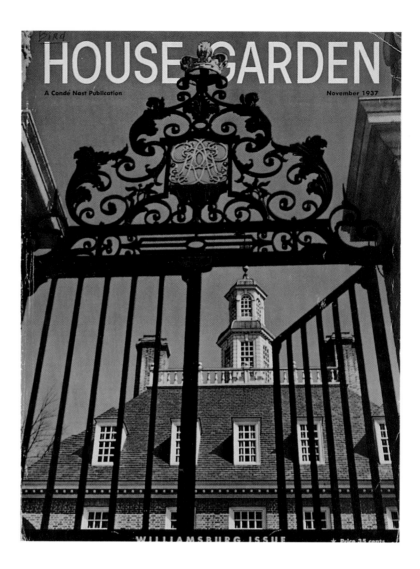

HOUSE GARDEN
A Condé Nast Publication   November 1937

WILLIAMSBURG ISSUE   ★ Price 35 cents

Cover of the Williamsburg issue of *House and Garden*, November 1937, showing the recently reconstructed Governor's Palace

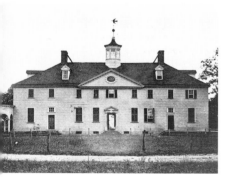

Mount Vernon, the first historic home conscientiously preserved in 19th-century America, 1860

Looking Back

T HE DESIRE TO RESTORE AND PRESERVE historic homes dates back to the 19th century, when patriotism led people to safeguard those buildings linked to the nation's political history, such as the homes of presidents George Washington and Andrew Jackson. Beginning as early as 1876, the Colonial Revival generated a broader appreciation for Georgian- and Federal-style houses. The restoration and reconstruction of historic sites such as Colonial Williamsburg in the late 1920s was a manifestation of this interest in historic buildings. During the 1930s, the federal government's Historic American Buildings Survey put thousands of unemployed architects, draftsmen, and writers to work documenting historic sites, further enhancing public appreciation of America's architectural heritage. In addition to this program, the establishment of historic districts like the one in Charleston, South Carolina, created

Love Affair with the Past

An old house is a state of mind.
THE OLD-HOUSE JOURNAL, JANUARY 1974 [1]

Since the 1960s, do-it-yourself home improvement has been influenced by a growing interest in the "old." Over the course of several decades, as historic houses and their restoration have moved from being a preoccupation of a small group of wealthy specialists to a fascination of ordinary Americans, homeowners have increasingly remodeled their dwellings with an eye to the past. The 1960s historic-preservation movement, a rising interest in craftsmanship, and nostalgia for the past have all contributed to this popular preference for old and old-looking homes.

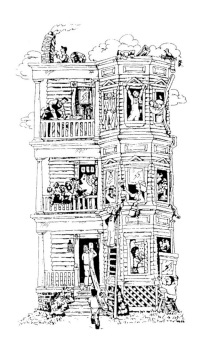

Illustration from the newsletter
of the Boston Preservation Alliance,
an organization promoting grassroots
interest in historic preservation, 1992

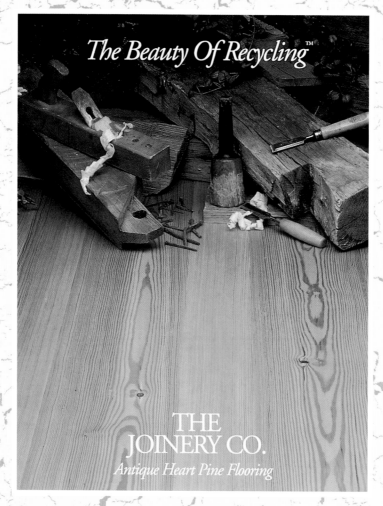

The Beauty Of Recycling™

THE
JOINERY CO.
Antique Heart Pine Flooring

TOP The Joinery Company found a market for pine flooring milled of timber salvaged from 19th-century buildings, 1990.

PREVIOUS PAGE North Carolina homeowners Judy and Fred Stokes measuring boards for repairs to a floor in their 19th-century farm-house, 1988

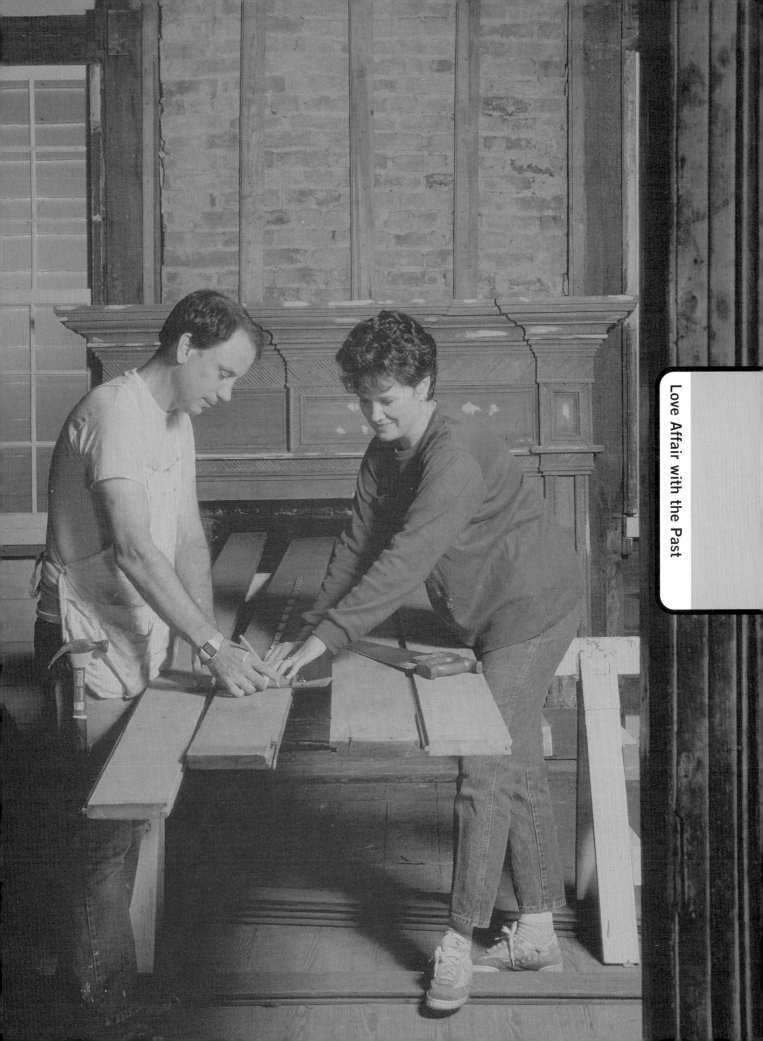

Love Affair with the Past

in 1931, helped extend popular ideas about preservation to include domestic structures of less than national interest. Shelter magazines such as *House and Garden* and *House Beautiful* supported the trend by endorsing simpler revival house forms, like the Cape Cod, and highlighting their compatibility with the priorities of modern architecture and interior design.[2]

THE 1960S HISTORIC-PRESERVATION MOVEMENT built on the foundation of the Colonial Revival and brought national attention to old houses for new reasons. Responding in part to the perceived dehumanization of American cities by modern architecture and large-scale urban-renewal projects, preservationists used education and advocacy to prevent the destruction of old buildings. The National Trust for Historic Preservation, a private, nonprofit organization established in 1949, brought preservation to national attention as it gained momentum and greater visibility in the 1960s. By sponsoring Preservation Week (beginning in 1973), acquiring historic properties, and publishing a monthly newsletter and a bimonthly magazine, the National Trust led a drive to rehabilitate old and historic buildings as part of the revitalization of many cities. The organization also helped communities throughout the country work at the grassroots level to encourage the purchase and restoration of historic buildings. The National Historic Preservation Act of 1966 provided government funding for the National Trust, as well as many state preservation programs, enhancing the organizations' ability to promote their agendas.[3]

THE NATIONAL TRUST'S LEADERSHIP RESULTED in a number of changes that predisposed Americans to work toward preserving historic properties. On the local level, the formation of neighborhood groups, preservation boards, and historic districts encouraged, and sometimes required, homeowners to improve their homes in ways that were sensitive to the historic character of their neighborhoods. Tax incentives for rehabilitating commercially used historic properties and landmark designations protecting culturally significant properties also prompted many business owners and entrepreneurs to consider renovating older structures. By 1977 there were more than four thousand historic-preservation organizations in the United States. These grassroots organizations devised strategies for obtaining landmark status for buildings and taught adaptive reuse techniques.[4]

AN INCREASED APPRECIATION FOR CRAFTSMANSHIP in the 1970s also fueled the popularization of restoration among homeowners. Handmade goods of all kinds were highly desirable to middle-class baby-boomers, who had been raised in a prosperous era of mass production. As young adults during the 1960s counterculture movement, many members of this generation questioned the technocratic and consumerist focus of modern life.[5] To varying degrees and in

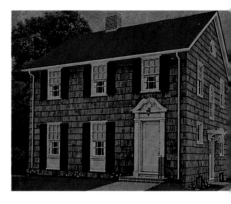

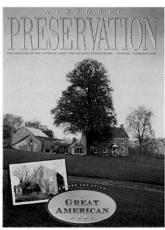

FAR TOP This typical suburban Colonial Revival house anachronistically combined elements from different historic architectural styles, 1928.

TOP Preserving the idea of "before" and "after": the cover of *Historic Preservation* magazine, January/February 1996, which featured the National Trust's annual Great American Home Awards

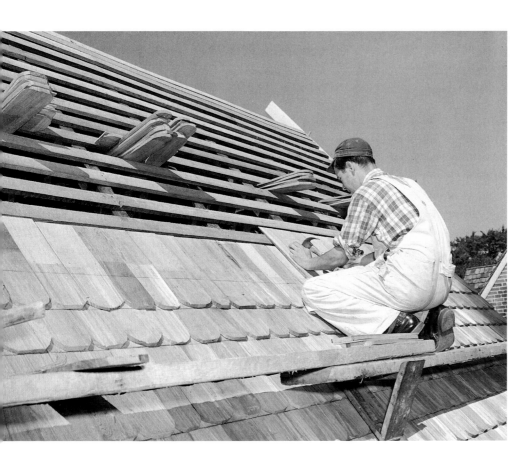

Installation of replacement wooden
roof shingles on the Brush-Everard
House, Colonial Williamsburg, 1950

many different ways, they rejected the suburban ideal as artificial
and inauthentic. Dismissing "cookie-cutter" houses — or, as song-
writer Malvina Reynolds put it, "Little Boxes"— along with other
mass-marketed goods, some took up residence in inner-city neighborhoods in search of alternative sources of community. For those who
advocated a wiser, more responsible use of environmental resources,
the preservation of old houses represented a sort of recycling.
Economic recession and the 1970s oil embargo and energy crisis
further encouraged urban homesteaders to "rehab" houses in mar-
ginal or declining areas. How-to manuals such as *The Whole Earth
Catalog* (first published in 1969) provided them with instructions
in manual skills such as growing their own food, enabling them to
achieve a measure of self-sufficiency and independence from
corporate-driven consumer culture.[6]

JUST AS MANY MIDDLE-CLASS AMERICANS had embraced the craftsman ideal at the turn of the century, so again in the 1970s did a
subsequent generation struggle to maintain a connection to the world
of production through reforming domestic living spaces. Some individuals rejected their parents' white-collar, professional careers to seek
employment involving manual work in such fields as carpentry, housebuilding, and architectural crafts. Many who did pursue office

jobs chose woodworking and housebuilding as leisure-time hobbies, imbuing them with particular seriousness and personal meaning.[7] Old houses suited the decade's emphasis on the skill and craftsmanship required for high-quality construction and ornamental detail.

THE APPEAL OF OLD HOUSES, and houses remodeled to appear old, also stemmed from a more general nostalgia for the past. Originally the term "nostalgia" referred to homesickness, a severe disease that overcame individuals removed from family and place of origin for long periods of time.[8] In its colloquial sense today, nostalgia still conveys a longing for home, as well as for an ideal past. Dramatic social and political change in the 1960s and 1970s, combined with the threat of nuclear war, led many to question America's post-World War II optimism about the future. Increasingly in recent decades, Americans have looked to older houses — as well as antique furniture, clothing, and other objects — as a way to connect with an imagined less-troubled past.

HOW INDIVIDUALS CHOSE TO ACHIEVE an old effect depended, of course, on available time and money. Wealthy families reclaimed old houses and hired expert craftsmen to restore them in elaborate, labor-intensive ways. They drew on the availability of specialists in traditional building arts who had gained experience by working on large public restoration projects. Plaster ornament, decorative ironwork, slate roofs, and custom-designed interior woodwork were among the specialty jobs purchased to bring back the original flair and elegance of large estates.

MIDDLE-CLASS FAMILIES STUDIED upper-class examples in magazines, looking for ways to execute restoration projects on their own. Many of the effects they desired required special skills that fell outside the realm of the amateur builder. Limited resources and a passion for fine craftsmanship motivated many do-it-yourselfers to learn the skills of the expert building craftsmen. Restoration became synonymous with gentrification, as families contributed newly acquired skills as "sweat equity" to enhance the value of brownstones and bungalows in urban neighborhoods.

BY THE MID-1970S, a new array of instructional venues for restoration procedures emerged to address homeowners' growing interest in traditional building skills. Heartwood Homebuilding Workshops of Washington, Massachusetts began offering a course in timber framing. The Historical Workshops at Eastfield in Nassau, New York launched training for restoration enthusiasts in traditional flatwall plastering as well as in procedures for casting plaster cornices and medallions.[9] Courses like these, plus the widespread popularity of woodworking hobbies, had the cumulative effect of elevating the ability of many home craftspeople to emulate restoration specialists.

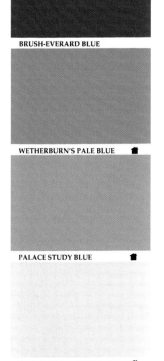

BRUSH-EVERARD BLUE

WETHERBURN'S PALE BLUE ■

PALACE STUDY BLUE ■

PALACE DINING ROOM PEARL BLUE ■

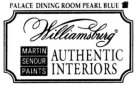

SIMULATED WHITEWASH

RALEIGH TAVERN CHINESE RED

*Authentic Colonial Colors...
for Today's Lifestyle.* W-13
■ *also available in exterior*

Paint-chip card of six Williamsburg paint colors, 1986

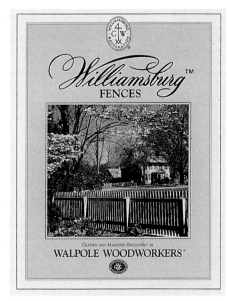

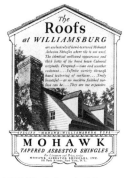

LEFT The hallmark of the Williamsburg Products Program appears on all reproduction materials licensed by Colonial Williamsburg, Inc.

TOP Roofing advertisement printed in *House and Garden's* Williamsburg issue, November 1937

Ye Olde Marketplace

THE SAME MARKETPLACE THAT RESPONDED to the interest in do-it-yourself projects in the 1950s and 1960s capitalized on popular interest in the old by offering an array of products for such tasks as stripping paint, reproducing or matching original moldings, and replacing tin ceilings. Many of these products, which were originally developed for the restoration of nationally important historic buildings in the first half of the century, have become available to homeowners in recent decades. The home-improvement marketplace has transformed to allow more people to incorporate old—or at least old-seeming—elements into their remodeling projects. Products range from reproductions of old wallpapers, paints, and antique hardware to high-tech power tools that make it possible to achieve elaborate woodworking effects with little effort. CUSTOM SUPPLIES FOR RESTORING OLD HOUSES were developed as early as the 1930s, when manufacturers worked with curators at Colonial Williamsburg to produce an array of materials for restoring the historic site. By the middle of the decade, Colonial Williamsburg applied its motto—"that the Future may learn from the Past"—to support the mass-marketing of these products to homeowners interested in renovating their old houses with some degree of historical accuracy. For example, Mohawk Asbestos Shingles, Inc. designed concrete tiles with asbestos binder to emulate wooden shingles on original roofs and advertised them in a special 1937 Williamsburg issue of *House and Garden*. Through analysis of the extant 18th-century structures in the historic Virginia town, researchers also

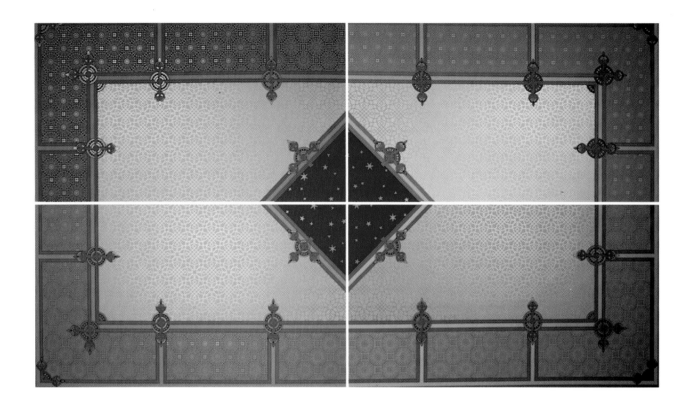

established a set of paint colors dating from the period. Over time, the successful sale of these paints sparked Colonial Williamsburg to release other "approved reproductions" of such architectural products as wallpaper, interior tile, molding, and fences.[10]

RECENT DECADES HAVE ALSO SEEN the establishment of a number of small restoration-oriented businesses catering to a growing niche market. For example, Bradbury and Bradbury started reproducing historical wallpapers in the late 1980s. Today the company offers a range of patterns, including exact reproductions, adaptations, and contemporary interpretations of historic styles.

EQUIPMENT AND MATERIALS MANUFACTURERS RESPONDED to the interest in old and old-looking houses with new lines of sophisticated tools and supplies. For example, detail-sanding power tools, introduced in the early 1990s, enabled quicker achievement of period effects. With accessory scraper attachments, they allowed for careful and accurate paint removal on elements such as aging moldings. Other products introduced for restoration work included epoxy systems for restoring rotted wood that would otherwise need to be replaced altogether.

FOR THE LESS-SKILLED INDIVIDUAL, a variety of ready-made restoration products have made it easier to achieve classical and Victorian decorative effects. Precut wooden moldings make it possible to recreate and install old-seeming interior fittings without special

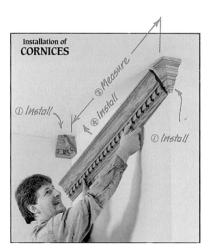

FAR TOP Ceiling wallpaper by Bradbury and Bradbury in the design vocabulary of 19th-century English designer Christopher Dresser

TOP Cornice installation simplified by a ready-made product. The need for the homeowner to have a high level of woodworking knowledge or skill has been eliminated, 1994.

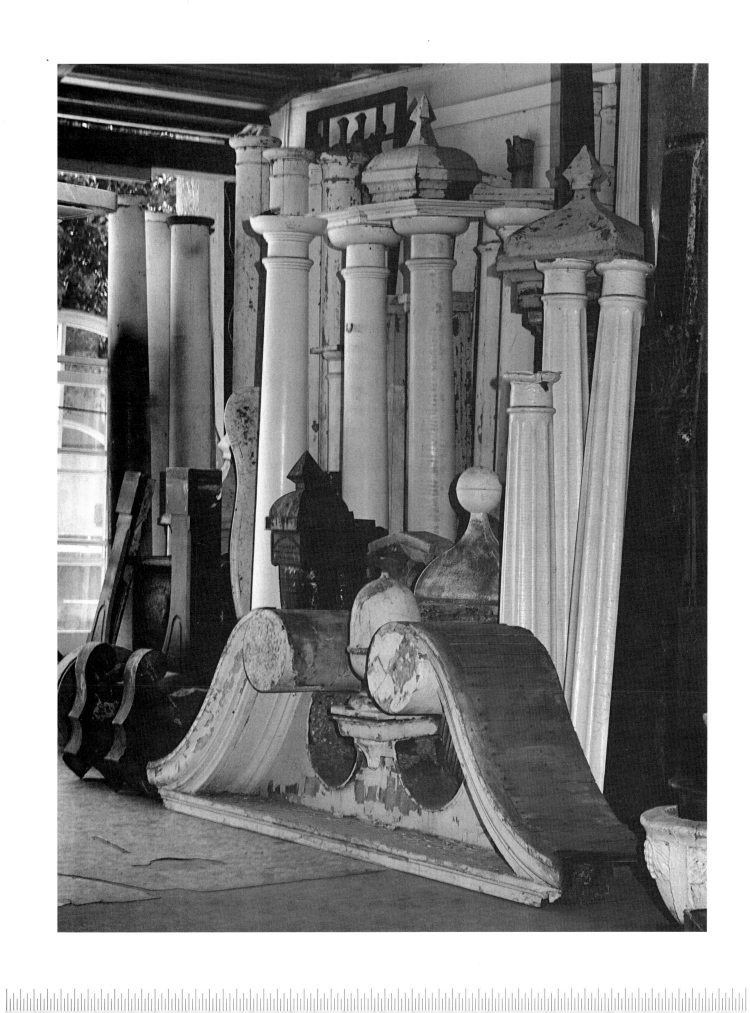

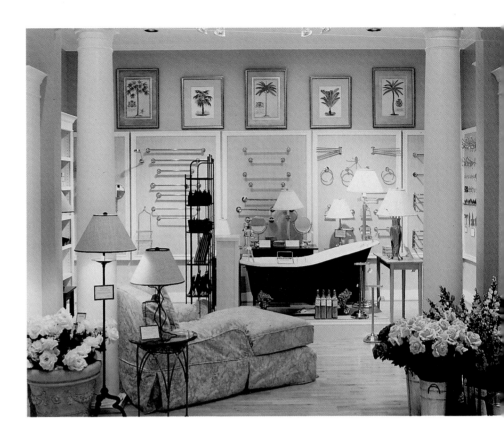

OPPOSITE PAGE Architectural
salvage awaiting sale at the
Backdoors Warehouse, Washington,
D.C., 1995

RIGHT Interior of Restoration
Hardware, ca. 1996

woodworking know-how or tools, while imitation moldings and
ornamental "plasterwork" made of polyurethane and plastic offer
the look of something old, but require little time or effort.
A RANGE OF RETAIL OUTLETS have emerged to sell these types of
restoration products. Salvage yards have become popular places to
find authentic architectural components, and mail-order sources
such as the *American Historical Supply Catalogue* (initiated in 1984)
offer reproduction building supplies, hardware, and other fixtures as
well as furniture and housewares. In recent years, true old-house
enthusiasts have been able to explore the full range of possibilities at
such large-scale events as "Restoration," a traveling trade show
where paying participants can attend demonstrations and peruse the
latest restoration-related paints, hardware, and decorative materials.
In addition, Restoration Hardware, a national chain of retail boutiques
catering to an upper-middle-class market, has offered a selection
of historically inspired artifacts —"antique" tools and reproduction
fixtures—for the home. The store's interior design and display
system, featuring anecdotal labels, makes shopping for these goods
a nostalgic experience in itself.[11] At the same time, ordinary hardware
stores, home centers, and home warehouses have expanded to
include many restoration-related goods among their general home-
improvement supplies.

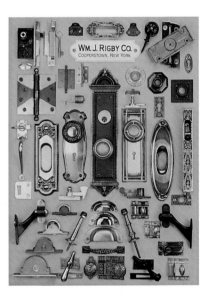

Advertisement for the
Wm. J. Rigby Company, a purveyor
since 1993 of original late-19th-
and early-20th-century builder's
hardware, 1997

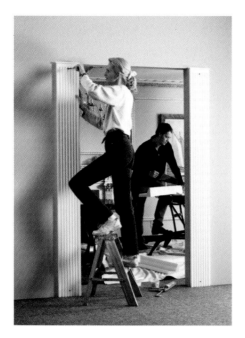 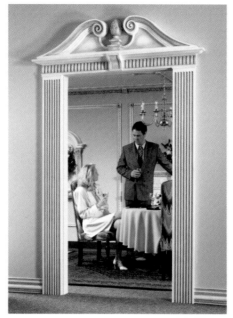

Do-it-yourself elegance created through the use of polyurethane — rather than plaster or wood — ornament, 1997

THE MEDIA JOINED IN TO PROMOTE a popular interest in restoration and craftsmanship, with new books and magazines addressing the growing desire among private individuals to restore old homes. In 1973 a monthly newsletter *The Old-House Journal: Restoration and Maintenance Techniques for the Antique House* began featuring regular articles on stripping and refinishing old floors, repairing old plasterwork, and rebuilding old stairs. General how-to instruction books such as the *Reader's Digest Home Improvements Manual* also began addressing issues of old house restoration and related skills. *Historic Preservation* magazine's "Workshop" column, started in 1983 and later called "Homeworks," provided a question-and-answer forum to air concerns about "restoration and renovation."[12]

THE CELEBRATION OF OLD HOMES secured its place in mainstream American culture perhaps most decisively with its appearance on television. The inauguration of *This Old House* on PBS in 1979 provided viewers with a weekly opportunity to watch renovation processes unfold before their very eyes. Focusing on one or two houses per season, the show demonstrated how dilapidated old structures could be transformed in ways that were sensitive to their historic integrity. The television program's immediate success signaled a curiosity about livable alternatives to building new. By providing detailed step-by-step explanations of processes, *This Old House* makes many tasks seem accessible to the novice while also promoting an appreciation for professional craftsmanship as well as regional and historic house styles. The television program, and since 1995 its spin-off magazine, do not adhere to any single definition of restora-

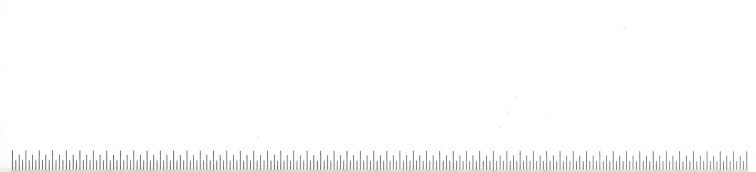

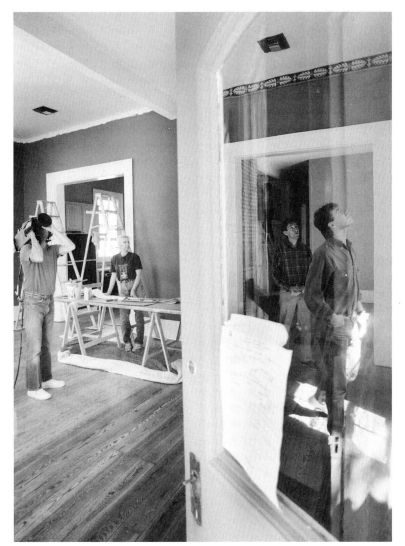

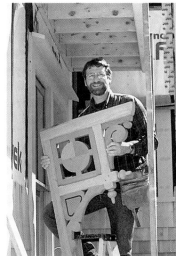

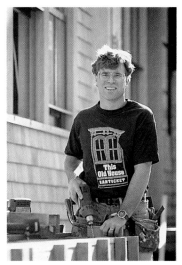

tion, choosing instead to show old and new techniques, materials, and effects with equal enthusiasm. *This Old House* serves as an important vehicle for Americans interested in old houses to explore home-improvement choices.

THE SUCCESS OF NEWER TELEVISION PROGRAMS and magazines seeking to emulate the general format of *This Old House* suggests that the combined interest in restoration and renovation remains on the rise today. American homeowners are attracted to the old for a complex set of reasons. Their love affair with the past is tempered by a desire for modern standards of comfort and convenience, values which have been central to the popularity of home improvement since the beginning of the 20th century. As each family continues to approach home remodeling according to its needs and priorities, all contribute to an ongoing process of defining and redefining a place for do-it-yourself in American culture.

CLOCKWISE FROM TOP LEFT

This Old House uses television to present dramatic stories about real people renovating old houses, 1991.

Norm Abram, master carpenter on the public television program *This Old House*, installing a carved bracket, Nantucket, 1996

Steve Thomas, host of *This Old House*, 1996

NOTES

BEFORE AND AFTER

1. "New Things and Old," *Hobbies* (March 1933): 7, quoted in Steven M. Gelber, "A Job You Can't Lose: Work and Hobbies in the Great Depression," *Journal of Social History* 24 (Summer 1991): 743.

2. Steven M. Gelber, "Do-It-Yourself: Constructing, Repairing and Maintaining Domestic Masculinity," *American Quarterly* 49 (March 1997): 66–112; T. J. Jackson Lears, *No Place of Grace* (New York: Pantheon, 1981), Chapter 2; Wendy Kaplan, ed., *The Art that is Life: The Arts and Crafts Movement in America, 1875–1920* (Boston: Little Brown, 1987); Eileen Cynthia Boris, *Art and Labor: John Ruskin, William Morris, and the Craftsman Ideal in America, 1876–1915* (Philadelphia: Temple University Press, 1986); John R. Stilgoe, *Borderland: Origins of the American Suburb, 1820–1939* (New Haven: Yale University Press, 1988), 260–69.

3. Garrett Winslow, "Practical Decoration for the Home Interior," *Suburban Life* 15 (November 1912): 187, cited in Gelber, "Do-It-Yourself," 79.

4. On *Popular Mechanics*, see Joseph J. Corn, "Educating the Enthusiast: Print and the Popularization of Technical Knowledge," in *Possible Dreams: Enthusiasm for Technology in America*, edited by John L. Wright (Dearborn, MI: Henry Ford Museum & Greenfield Village, 1992), 18–33.

5. Gelber, "A Job You Can't Lose," 741–66.

6. *Sears, Roebuck and Company Catalog* (Fall 1901): 968; *Sears, Roebuck and Company Catalog* (Fall 1905): 681–83; *Sears, Roebuck and Company Catalog* (Spring 1903): 903. On Sears and other mail-order catalogs, see Susan Strasser, *Satisfaction Guaranteed: The Making of the American Mass Market* (New York: Pantheon, 1989), 212–16.

7. *Sears, Roebuck and Company Catalog* (Fall 1905): 352; *Sears, Roebuck and Company Catalog* (Spring 1920): 1250.

8. *House and Garden Modernization Portfolio* (1938): 23.

9. Clifford Edward Clark, Jr., *The American Family Home, 1800–1960* (Chapel Hill: University of North Carolina Press, 1986); Gwendolyn Wright, *Moralism and the Model Home: Domestic Architecture and Cultural Conflict in Chicago, 1873–1913* (Chicago: University of Chicago Press, 1980); Jan Jennings, "Drawing on the Vernacular Interior," *Winterthur Portfolio* 27 (Winter 1992): 255–79; and "Controlling Passion: The Turn-of-the-Century Wallpaper Dilemma," *Winterthur Portfolio* 31 (Winter 1996): 243–64; Herbert Gottfried, "Building the Picture: Trading on the Imagery of Production and Design," *Winterthur Portfolio* 27 (Winter 1992): 235–53; Stuart Blumin, *The Emergence of the Middle Class: Social Experience in the American City, 1760–1900* (Cambridge, England and New York: Cambridge University Press, 1989).

10. Frank L. Mott, *A History of American Magazines*, vol. 5, (Cambridge, MA: Harvard University Press, 1968), 43.

11. Frederick C. Hitch, "The Transformation of a 'Modern' House," *House Beautiful* 47 (January 1920): 17.

12. Thomas C. Jester, ed., *Twentieth-Century Building Materials: History and Conservation* (New York: McGraw-Hill, 1995), 269–71.

13. Ruth Schwartz Cowan, *More Work for Mother: The Ironies of Household Technology from the Open Hearth to the Microwave* (New York: Basic Books, 1983); Susan Strasser, *Never Done: A History of American Housework* (New York: Pantheon, 1982); Ellen Lupton and J. Abbott Miller, *The Bathroom, the Kitchen, and the Aesthetics of Waste: A Process of Elimination* (New York: Kiosk/Princeton Architectural Press, 1992); Suellen Hoy, *Chasing Dirt: The American Pursuit of Cleanliness* (New York: Oxford University Press, 1995).

14. Pamela H. Simpson, *Cheap, Quick and Easy: Imitative Architectural Materials, 1870–1930* (Knoxville, TN: University of Tennessee Press, forthcoming), Chapter 5; Bonnie Parks Snyder, "Linoleum," in Jester, ed., *Twentieth-Century Building Materials*, 215–21; Hazel Dell Brown, *The Attractive Home, How to Plan its Decoration* (Lancaster, PA: Armstrong Bureau of Interior Decoration, 1928).

15. "18,500,000 Gallons of Paint," *Fortune* 12 (August 1935): 83.

16. Janet Hutchison, "Building for Babbitt: The State and the Suburban Home Ideal," *Journal of Policy History* 9 (1997): 15–27.

17. Gelber, "Do-It-Yourself," 81.

18. Record Group 31, National Archives and Records Administration, Washington, D.C., sound recording 3, part 2.

19. *The FHA Story in Summary 1934–1959* (Washington, D.C.: Federal Housing Administration, 1959), 8.

20. *Sixth Annual Report of the Federal Housing Administration* (Washington, D.C.: Government Printing Office, 1940), 87.

21. Ronald C. Tobey, *Technology as Freedom: The New Deal and the Electrical Modernization of the American Home* (Berkeley: University of California Press, 1996), 107–09, 137–38.

22. Theodore E. Damm, "How the Paint Manufacturer Can Profit from the National Housing Act," *Oil, Paint, and Drug Reporter* (21 October 1935): 27.

23. Record Group 31, National Archives and Records Administration, Washington, D.C. contains nine separate "Better Housing News Flashes" released between 1934 and 1936.

THE AGE OF DO-IT-YOURSELF

1. "The New Do-It-Yourself Market," *Business Week* (14 June 1952): 60.

2. Captain Alfred Friendly, "'Almost Good Enough' Won't Be Good Enough For Him," *House Beautiful* (January 1945): 81.

3. Donald Albrecht, ed., *World War II and the American Dream: How Wartime Building Changed a Nation* (Washington, D.C.: National Building Museum; Cambridge, MA: MIT Press, 1995); Greg Hise, *Magnetic Los Angeles: Planning the Twentieth-Century Metropolis* (Baltimore: Johns Hopkins University Press, 1997); Harry B. Leut, *Seabee Bill Scott Builds and Fights for the Navy* (New York: MacMillan, 1944).

4. Friendly, "'Almost Good Enough,'" 38–39, 81, 90, 92.

5. "Repair for Defense," *American Home* (March 1942): 94–95; *House Beautiful Maintenance and Postwar Building Manual* (New York: Hearst Magazines, 1944).

6. John Morton Blum, *V Was for Victory: Politics and American Culture during World War II* (New York: Harcourt Brace Jovanovich, 1976), 102.

7. Albrecht, ed., *World War II and the American Dream*, xli; "The New Do-It-Yourself

Market," 61; Elaine Tyler May, *Homeward Bound: American Families in the Cold War Era* (New York: Basic Books, 1988), 163.

8. May, *Homeward Bound*, 78; Clark, *The American Family Home*, 227; James B. Gilbert, *Another Chance: Postwar America, 1945–1985* (Belmont, CA: Wadsworth Publishing, Inc.: 1986), 22–23; Karal Ann Marling, *As Seen on TV: The Visual Culture of Everyday Life in the 1950s* (Cambridge, MA: Harvard University Press. 1994), 51–52.

9. "5,500 Houses," *Fortune* (March 1938): 100-110; Barbara M. Kelly, *Expanding the American Dream: Building and Rebuilding Levittown* (Albany: State University of New York, 1993).

10. Herbert J. Gans, *The Levittowners: Ways of Life and Politics in a New Suburban Community* (New York: Pantheon, 1967). On similar trends in Canada, see Annmarie Adams and Pieter Sijpkes, "Wartime Housing and Architectural Change, 1942–1992," *Canadian Folklore* 17, no. 2 (1995): 13–29.

11. Surveys by *Better Homes and Gardens* and Department of Commerce, Housing and Home Finance Agency, cited in Clark, *The American Family Home*, 228–30.

12. *Better Homes and Gardens* (October 1951): 193.

13. "The New Do-It-Yourself Market," 60.

14. Ibid, 61.

15. May, *Homeward Bound*, 165–66.

16. On the culture of leisure in the 1950s, see Marling, *As Seen on TV*, 51–53.

17. Darrell Huff, "We've Found a Substitute for Income," *Harper's* (October 1953): 27.

18. William Whyte, *The Organization Man* (New York: Simon and Schuster, 1956); David Riesman, with Reuel Denney and Nathan Glazer, *The Lonely Crowd: A Study of the Changing American Character* (New Haven: Yale University Press, 1950); C. Wright Mills, *White Collar: The American Middle Class* (New York: Oxford University Press, 1951); Albert Roland, "Do-It-Yourself: A Walden for the Millions?" *American Quarterly* 10 (Summer 1958): 154–64.

19. "Do-It-Yourself Takes Over," *McCall's* (January 1955): 24.

20. Mary L. Seelhorst, "Ninety Years of Popular Mechanics," in Wright, ed., *Possible Dreams*, 85–86.

21. *Better Homes and Gardens Handyman's Book* (Des Moines: Meredith Publishing Company, 1951).

22. "The New Do-It-Yourself Market," 70.

23. John Keats, *The Crack in the Picture Window* (Boston: Houghton Mifflin, 1956), 73–74.

24. Bill Mauldin, *Life* (25 July 1955): 94–96, 99–100, 102. See also Bill Mauldin, *Up Front* (New York: Henry Holt and Company, 1945) and *Back Home* (New York: William Sloane Associates, 1947); and Frederick S. Voss, *Reporting the War* (Washington, D.C.: Smithsonian Institution Press, 1994), 109–17.

25. "*Life* Clobbers Do-It-Yourself Homeowners," *Family Handyman* (November 1955): 15.

THE DO-IT-YOURSELF MARKETPLACE

1. *Better Homes and Gardens Handyman's Book*, 201.

2. "The New Do-It-Yourself Market," 69; and "The Shoulder Trade," *Time* (2 August 1954): 62–68.

3. "The New Do-It-Yourself Market," 72, 74; and *Home-Utility Electric Tools* (Towson, Maryland: The Black & Decker Manufacturing Company, 1949).

4. See, for example, "A $245.00 Workshop Complete For Only $96.75—Built With My Skil Home Shop Tools," *Popular Mechanics* (October 1951): 293; and "New Porter-Cable Homemaster 1/4" Drill," *Popular Science* (October 1954): 259.

5. Elbert Robberson, "What You Should Know About Buying an Electric Drill," *Popular Science* (March 1954).

6. "Dr. G's Motorized Tool Kit," *Popular Science* (March 1950): 164–71.

7. See "Ask for a Rockwell-Built Delta-Shop for a Christmas of a Lifetime," *Popular Science* (December 1954): 229; and "Give Yourself a Power Workshop," *Better Homes and Gardens* (December 1950): 166, 177–79.

8. "The New Look in Home Power Tools," *Business Week* (20 March 1954), 150–52; and Paul Corey and Darrell Huff, "Deluxe Power Tool Whips Out Homework," *Popular Science* (April 1954): 176–81.

9. Robert Friedel, "Scarcity and Promise: Materials and American Domestic Culture during World War II," in Albrecht, ed., *World War II and the American Dream*, 42–89; and Jester, ed., *Twentieth-Century Building Materials*, 132–35.

10. "The New Do-It-Yourself Market," 62.

11. Herb Pfister and Harry Walton, "You Can Use Aluminum like Wood," *Popular Science* (December 1953): 159–67; and *Reynolds Aluminum and the*

Company That Makes It (Louisville, KY: Reynolds Metals Company, 1956), 68–69.

12. *Basic Wiring: A Money-Saving Guide to Electrical Repairs and Renovations Inside Your Home and Out* (Alexandria, Va.: Time-Life Books, 1976); and *Reader's Digest Complete Do-It-Yourself Manual* (Pleasantville, NY: Reader's Digest Association, Inc., 1973), 261.

13. *The Family Handyman Encyclopedia: The Do-It-Yourself Guide* (Universal Publishing and Book Distributing Corporation, 1965), 540.

14. *The 1953 Home Decorator and How-to-Paint Book* (Cleveland: The Sherwin-Williams Company, 1953), 9.

15. "War Paint Stays," *Business Week* (4 May 1946): 73–74; and "Mix Paints Go To Town," *Business Week* (14 February 1948): 58, 63.

16. "Paint for Brush-loving Amateurs," *Modern Packaging* 16 (October 1942): 64–65.

17. Terry Armstrong, "Record Breaker in Paint: The Sales and Advertising Story Behind Kem-Tone," *Sales Management* 53 (15 October 1944): 23–26.

18. "The New Do-It-Yourself Market," 62.

19. "Paint for Brush-loving Amateurs," 64–65. On paint rollers, see also "Rolling Up Roller Sales," *Business Week* (10 January 1953): 83, 86, 88, 89; and "To Paint with a Roller or a Brush?" *Consumers' Research Bulletin* 37 (February 1956): 23–24.

20. "American Home in Review," *Printers' Ink Monthly* (April 1940): 38.

21. "Now—famous Imperial Washable Wallpapers come to you trimmed and pasted!" advertisement in *House Beautiful* (March 1954): 217.

22. "The New Do-It-Yourself Market," 66; and "The Wonderful Ways of Wallpaper," *House Beautiful* (March 1954): 121–23.

23. Jeffrey L. Meikle, *American Plastic: A Cultural History* (New Brunswick: Rutgers University Press, 1995), 184, 256–57.

24. Jester, ed. *Twentieth-Century Building Materials*, 135.

25. Jonathan Aley, "Super Markets For the Amateur Handyman," *American Home* 54 (August 1955): 22.

26. Huff, "We've Found a Substitute for Income," 30.

27. See Vince Staten, *Did Monkeys Invent the Monkey Wrench? Hardware Stores and Hardware Stories* (New York: Simon and Schuster, 1996).

28. "The Building of America," *Do-It-Yourself Retailing* (June 1986): 82.

29. Ibid., 86–95.

30. "Hardware Store Takes to Supermarket Way," *Business Week* (8 September 1956): 76.

31. Jeffrey Rodengen, *The Legend of Stanley: 150 Years of the Stanley Works* (Fort Lauderdale, FL: Write Stuff Syndicate, Inc., 1996), 96.

32. "Build It Yourself," *Business Week* (18 October 1956): 52.

33. See the records of the National Retail Lumber Dealers Association and issues of the association journal, *The Plan,* at Hagley Museum and Library, Wilmington, Delaware.

34. "The Building of America," 99, 102; Edward R. Kantowicz, *True Value: John Cotter 70 Years of Hardware* (Chicago: Regnery Books, 1986); and Cheri Carpenter, *The Place is Ace: The History of Ace Hardware* (Oak Brook, Illinois: Ace Hardware Corporation, 1992).

35. Burt Murphy, "The Home Improvement Market," *Mechanix Illustrated* 78 (March 1982): 8.

36. Jay Gissen, "Nice Number, 40,000," *Forbes* (21 November 1983), 292. On Lowe's, see Dan McIntyre, *No Place Like Lowe's: 50 Years of Retailing for the American Home* (North Wilkesboro, NC: Lowe's Companies, Inc., 1996).

37. "The Building of America," 107.

38. *The Home Depot 1996 Annual Report* (Atlanta: The Home Depot, Inc., 1997).

39. For a survey of today's marketplace, see The Editors of *This Old House Magazine*, *This Old House Sourcebook* (Boston: Little, Brown and Company, 1997).

HANDYMAN, HANDYWOMAN

1. "House Building and Home Making," *The House Beautiful* 38 (September 1915): 114.

2. Gilbert, *Another Chance,* 54–75; Gelber, "Do-It-Yourself," 90–97; May, *Homeward Bound*; and Joanne Meyerowitz, ed., *Not June Cleaver: Women and Gender in Postwar America, 1945–1960* (Philadelphia: Temple University Press, 1994).

3. "Do-It-Yourself Takes Over," *McCall's* (January 1955): 24.

4. *Better Homes and Gardens* (March 1939): 77.

5. Susan M. Hartmann, *The Home Front and Beyond: American Women in the 1940s* (Boston: Twayne Publishers, 1982); and Gilbert, *Another Chance*, 15.

6. *House Beautiful's Maintenance and Postwar Building Manual* (New York: Hearst Magazines, 1944).

7. May, *Homeward Bound*, 167.

8. "Can Your Wife Drive a Nail?" *American Magazine* (July 1950): 57; and Robert Hertzberg, "Manual Training for Housewives," *Popular Science* (August 1950): 201–03.

9. "Do-It-Yourself Takes Over," 24. See also Armstrong, "Record Breaker in Paint: The Sales and Advertising Story Behind Kem-Tone."

10. On women and cleanliness, see Hoy, *Chasing Dirt*; Strasser, *Never Done;* and Cowan, *More Work for Mother,* 88–89.

11. "Look at What You Can Do with a Drill in the Kitchen," *Popular Science* (June 1954): 228.

12. Stanley Tools advertisement, *Popular Mechanics* (October 1956): 2.

13. Ruth Oldenziel, "Gender and the Meanings of Technology: Engineering in the U.S., 1880–1945" (Ph.D. diss, Yale University, 1992).

14. Gelber, "Do-It-Yourself," 69.

15. Ibid., 66–112.

16. Rodengen, *The Legend of Stanley,* 95. See also Richard Nunn, "Hollywood Handymen," *Better Homes and Gardens* (November 1957): 44, quoted in Marling, *As Seen On TV*, 57.

17. Dick E. Wilson, "A Shower for the Bridegroom!" *American Magazine* (September 1954): 42–44, 62–65.

18. James L. A. Webb and Barton L. Houseman, *The You-Don't-Need-A-Man-To-Fix-It Book: The Woman's Guide to Confident Home Repair* (Garden City: Doubleday and Company, 1973), 2.

19. Florence Adams, *I Took A Hammer in My Hand: The Woman's Build-It and Fix-It Handbook* (New York: William Morrow & Company, Inc., 1973).

20. Webb and Houseman, *The You-Don't-Need-A-Man-To-*

Fix-It Book, 2. See also Barton L. Houseman and James L. A. Webb, *A Woman's Guide to Home Repair* (New York: Doubleday and Company, 1973); and Kay B. Ward, *The Feminine Fix-It Handbook: Everything You Need to Know to Do It Yourself* (New York: Grosset & Dunlap, 1972).

21. Schraub, "Home Centers," 48, 50, 52, 117.

22. Maryann Brinley, "Stores that Help you to be Handy," *McCall's* 110 (March 1983): 61–62.

23. Ibid.

LOVE AFFAIR WITH THE PAST

1. *The Old-House Journal* 2, no. 1 (January 1974): 2.

2. *House and Garden* 72, Williamsburg Issue (November 1937); Kenneth L. Ames, introduction to *The Colonial Revival in America*, edited by Alan Axelrod (New York: W. W. Norton and Company, 1985), 1–14; Karal Ann Marling, *George Washington Slept Here: Colonial Revivals and American Culture, 1876–1986* (Cambridge, MA: Harvard University Press, 1988).

3. Michael Wallace, "Reflections on the History of Historic Preservation," in *Presenting the Past: Essays on History and the Public*, edited by Susan Porter Benson, Stephen Brier, and Roy Rosenzweig (Philadelphia: Temple University Press, 1986), 165–199. On the National Trust, see Michael Kammen, *Mystic Chords of Memory: The Transformation of Tradition in American Culture* (New York: Alfred A. Knopf, 1991), 558–64, 613–14.

4. Kammen, *Mystic Chords of Memory*, 562–63.

5. William E. Leuchtenberg, *A Troubled Feast: American Society Since 1945* (Boston: Little, Brown and Co., 1973),

179–200; Gilbert, *Another Chance,* 263, 266–67.

6. Jane S. Becker and Barbara Franco, *Folk Roots, New Roots: Folklore in American Life* (Lexington, MA: Scottish Rite Masonic Museum and Library, 1988), 50–53. See also Charles Reich, *The Greening of America: How the Youth Revolution Is Trying to Make America Livable* (New York: Random House, 1970); David E. Shi, *The Simple Life: Plain Living and High Thinking in American Culture* (New York: Oxford University Press, 1985), 248–76; E. F. Schumacher, *Small is Beautiful: A Study of Economics as if People Mattered* (London: Blond and Briggs, 1973).

7. See the example of Jonathan Souweine and his wife Judith, in Tracy Kidder's *House* (Boston: Houghton Mifflin, 1985).

8. David Lowenthal, *The Past is a Foreign Country* (Cambridge, England: Cambridge University Press, 1985), 4–13.

9. Rick Mashburn, "A Restorer's Paradise: The New Product Explosion," *Historic Preservation* (May/June 1988): 58-63; Sally G. Oldham, "The Business of Preservation is Bullish and Diverse," *Preservation Forum* 3 no. 4 (Winter 1990): 14-19.

10. On Colonial Williamsburg in the 1930s, see *House and Garden* 72, Williamsburg Issue (November 1937). On historic paint colors, see Frank S. Welsh, "The Early American Palette: Colonial Paint Colors Revealed," in *Paint in America: The Colors of Historic Buildings*, edited by Roger W. Moss (Washington, D.C.: Preservation Press, National Trust for Historic Preservation), 70–71.

11. Michael Colton, "A Nuts and Bolts Boutique," *Washington Post* (23 June 1997); Patricia Leigh Brown, "A Hardware Store with an Ego," *New York Times* (20 February 1997).

12. See, for example, *Reader's Digest Home Improvements Manual* (Pleasantville, NY: Reader's Digest Association, 1982), 322–47. See also *Historic Preservation* (July–August 1983).

Administration. Courtesy E. I. du Pont de Nemours and Company, Inc.

40 left: Reprinted with permission from *Better Homes and Gardens®* magazine. ©Copyright Meredith Corporation 1997, All rights reserved.

40 right: Reprinted from *Popular Mechanics*, October 1951. ©Copyright the Hearst Corporation. All rights reserved.

41: Drawing by Saxon. ©1958 The New Yorker Magazine, Inc. All rights reserved.

42 top: Courtesy Roy Doty

42 bottom: Drawing by Claude. ©1960 The New Yorker Magazine, Inc. All rights reserved.

43 left (top, middle, and bottom): From Morris Brickman, *Do It Yourself* (New York: Gilbert Press, Inc., 1955)

43 right: Courtesy Bill Mauldin

44: From Morris Brickman, *Do It Yourself*, 1955

THE DO-IT-YOURSELF MARKETPLACE

45: Courtesy Archive Photos

46: Courtesy Shopsmith Inc.

48 all: Courtesy American Hardware Manufacturers Association

49 far top and top: Courtesy the Black & Decker Corporation

49 bottom: Courtesy Dremel

50 left: Courtesy the Black & Decker Corporation

50 top right: Courtesy Sears, Roebuck and Company

50 bottom right: Courtesy S-B Power Tool Company

51 left: Courtesy S-B Power Tool Company

51 top right: Courtesy the Black & Decker Corporation

51 bottom right: Courtesy Sears, Roebuck and Company

52–53 center: Reprinted with permission from *Better Homes and Gardens® Handyman's Book*. ©Copyright Meredith Corporation 1997. All rights reserved.

53 bottom left: Courtesy Reynolds Metals Company

53 bottom right: Courtesy National Gypsum Company

53 top right: Courtesy Weldwood of Canada Limited

54: Warshaw Collection of Business Americana, Archives Center, NMAH, Smithsonian Institution

55 left: ©The Sherwin-Williams Company. All rights reserved.

55 top right: Courtesy the Glidden Company

55 bottom right: Courtesy USG Corporation

56: Courtesy Sears, Roebuck and Company

57 top: Courtesy PPG Architectural Finishes Inc., a wholly owned subsidiary of PPG Industries, Inc.

57 bottom: Courtesy Fluid Management

58 top left: Courtesy Congoleum Corporation

58 bottom: Courtesy the Valspar Corporation

58 top right: Courtesy Kentile

59 left: Courtesy Commercial and Architectural Products, Inc.

59 middle: Richard Cheek Collection. Courtesy Kentile

59 right: Courtesy Armstrong World Industries, Inc.

60 top: Courtesy Sears, Roebuck and Company

60 bottom: Courtesy National Retail Hardware Association

61 top: Courtesy Ace Hardware Corporation

61 bottom: Wurts Brothers Collection, National Building Museum, Gift of Richard Wurts

62 top: Courtesy the Stanley Works. Photograph reproduced from Jeffrey L. Rodengen, *The Legend of Stanley: 150 Years of the Stanley Works*

62 bottom: Courtesy Genova Products

63 top: Courtesy TruServ Corporation

63 bottom: Hagley Museum and Library. Courtesy National Lumber and Building Material Dealers Association

64: Courtesy Home Depot

HANDYMAN, HANDYWOMAN

65: Record Group 306, National Archives and Records Administration. Courtesy E. I. du Pont de Nemours and Company

66: ©The Sherwin-Williams Company. All rights reserved.

67: From Morris Brickman, *Do It Yourself*, 1955

68 top: ©The Sherwin-Williams Company. All rights reserved.

68 bottom: Reprinted from *Popular Mechanics*, October 1953. ©Copyright the Hearst Corporation. All rights reserved.

69 top: Courtesy Johnson Controls, Inc.

69 bottom: Richard Cheek Collection. Reprinted from *House Beautiful Maintenance and Postwar Building Manual*, 1944. ©Copyright the Hearst Corporation. All rights reserved.

70 left: Reprinted from *The American Magazine*, July 1950

70 right: Record Group 306, National Archives and Records Administration. Courtesy General Electric Appliances

71 top left: Courtesy Columbus Coated Fabrics

71 bottom: Reprinted with permission from *Popular Science* magazine. Copyright 1950, Times Mirror Magazines Inc.

72: Courtesy PPG Architectural Finishes Inc., a wholly owned subsidiary of PPG Industries, Inc.

73: Richard Cheek Collection

74 top: Richard Cheek Collection. Courtesy Commercial and Architectural Products, Inc.

74 bottom: Reprinted with permission from *Better Homes and Gardens® Handyman's Book*. ©Copyright Meredith Corporation 1997. All rights reserved.

75 top right: Richard Cheek Collection. Reprinted from *Popular Mechanics Handyman's Guide Home Kinks*, 1942. ©Copyright the Hearst Corporation. All rights reserved.

75 bottom left: Reprinted with permission from *Popular Science* magazine. Copyright 1954, Times Mirror Magazines, Inc.

75 top left: Courtesy Ace Hardware Corporation

76 left: Courtesy Cooper Hand Tools Division of Cooper Industries

76 right: Courtesy Norfolk Southern Corporation

77 left: Courtesy Delta International Machinery Corporation.

77 right: Courtesy the Black & Decker Corporation

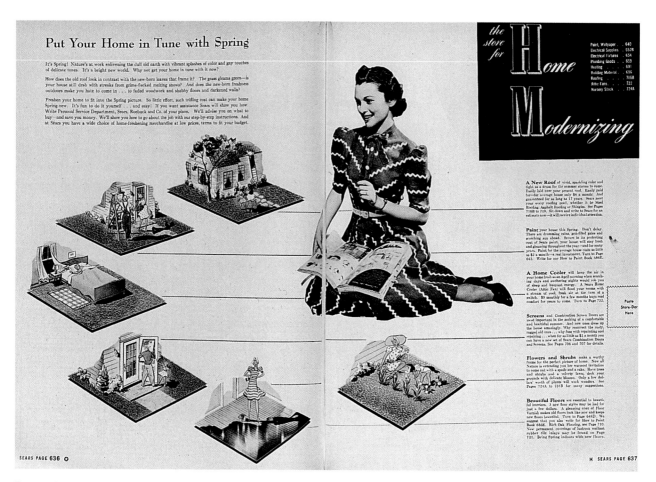

From the Sears, Roebuck and
Company catalog,
spring/summer, 1940

PREFACE

HOME IS AN OUTWARD EXPRESSION of who we are. Because we have a basic human desire to enhance the comfort and appearance of our environment, we alter our dwellings to reflect and confirm our identities.

THE AMERICAN OBSESSION WITH HOME IMPROVEMENT is the subject of *Do It Yourself*. It explores how generations of men and women have taken tools in hand to reconfigure spaces, repaint rooms, finish basements, redo kitchens and bathrooms, and fix leaking pipes. Importantly, it discusses this not only as a personal journey for homeowners but as a cultural phenomenon, in which manufacturers, retail companies, and the media all play roles in defining tastes and needs.

THE THEME OF SHAPING OUR WORLD is a recurrent one at the National Building Museum. Our exhibitions, educational programs, and publications examine the cultural, political, and technological forces that mold the built environment and the ways in which buildings affect and shape our lives. Located in a landmark building in Washington, D.C. and containing what Philip Johnson has called "the grandest interior space in America," the National Building Museum welcomes a national and international public and is fast becoming *the* forum for learning about the built environment.

THE AMERICAN HARDWARE MANUFACTURERS ASSOCIATION; the Graham Foundation for Advanced Studies in the Fine Arts; and Furthermore, the publication program of the J. M. Kaplan Fund, provided generous funding for the writing and design of this book. The Board of Trustees and I, as well as all our fine staff, are enormously grateful to them.

ADDITIONALLY, MANY PEOPLE AND ORGANIZATIONS contributed to *Do It Yourself*, and we are extremely grateful for their participation. Carolyn M. Goldstein brought boundless enthusiasm and informed vision to this book, and was ably assisted in her research by Michael R. Harrison and Jennifer Bride, with encouragement and support from Joseph Rosa.

I HOPE YOU ENJOY *Do It Yourself*. It provides powerful evidence of how we individualize our living spaces and transform house into home. Please come visit us soon at the National Building Museum.

Susan Henshaw Jones
President and Director
National Building Museum

OPPOSITE PAGE
New Yorker cartoonist Richard Taylor and Mrs. Robert Simpson helping to paint a home, Newtown, Connecticut, 1943

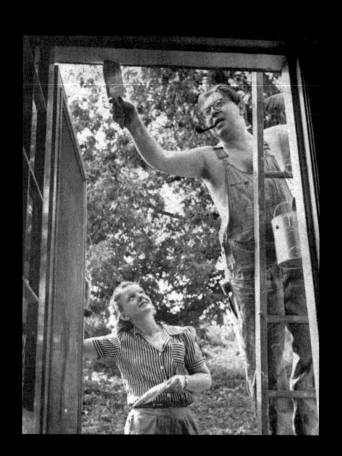

FOREWORD

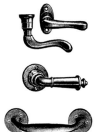

FOR MOST AMERICANS, a home is the investment of a lifetime. In part, that explains why millions of U.S. homeowners are so passionate about their do-it-yourself pursuits. This year, throughout our nation, consumers will spend more than $140 billion on home repair and remodeling products—but there's more to the story than protecting and enhancing an investment.

THE EVOLUTION OF THE DO-IT-YOURSELF PHENOMENON in this century, and its explosion after World War II, is interwoven into the social, economic, and political fabric of the United States. This book chronicles the development of the do-it-yourself concept in our culture.

WHAT MOTIVATES AMERICA'S LEGION of do-it-yourselfers? There are many different answers. For some, it's to save money. Others do it for the enjoyment and satisfaction of completing a home-related project. And for others still, it's "sweat equity."

THERE'S ALSO A NOSTALGIC ELEMENT to do-it-yourself. We recall holding the flashlight for Dad while he worked under the sink or helping Mom hang new wallpaper in the living room. Maybe it was accompanying Grandpa to the local hardware store, or trading tools and swapping "DIY war stories" with neighbors.

AS AN ORGANIZATION OF 1,100 U.S. FIRMS who make and market products destined for do-it-yourselfers, the American Hardware Manufacturers Association (AHMA) is delighted to see the story of do-it-yourself told in this publication. Since 1901, members of our group have been delivering the tools—literally and figuratively—that enable people to build on the American dream of homeownership.

William P. Farrell
President and CEO
American Hardware Manufacturers Association

CONTENTS

Published by
Princeton Architectural Press
37 East 7th Street
New York, New York 10003

and

National Building Museum
401 F Street NW
Washington, D.C. 20001

Printed and bound in the United States of America
03 02 01 00 99 98 97 5 4 3 2 1
First edition

Library of Congress Cataloging-in-Publication Data
Goldstein, Carolyn M., 1962–
Do it yourself: home improvement in 20th-century America / Carolyn M. Goldstein.
p.-cm.
Includes bibliographical references.
ISBN 1-56898-127-9 (alk. paper)
1. Dwellings—United States—Remodeling—
I. Title.
TH4816. G645-1998 97-46956
643'.7'074753—dc21 CIP

Additional support for this book was provided by the Graham Foundation for Advanced Studies in the Fine Arts and by Furthermore, the publication program of the J. M. Kaplan Fund.

Research Assistant: Michael R. Harrison

Book design:
J. Abbott Miller, Paul Carlos, Ji Byol Lee,
Design/Writing/Research

Book editor: Sara E. Stemen

Special thanks to: Eugenia Bell, Caroline Green, Clare Jacobson, Therese Kelly, Mark Lamster, and Annie Nitschke of Princeton Architectural Press
—Kevin C. Lippert, Publisher,
Princeton Architectural Press

For a complete catalog of books published by Princeton Architectural Press, call 800.722.6657

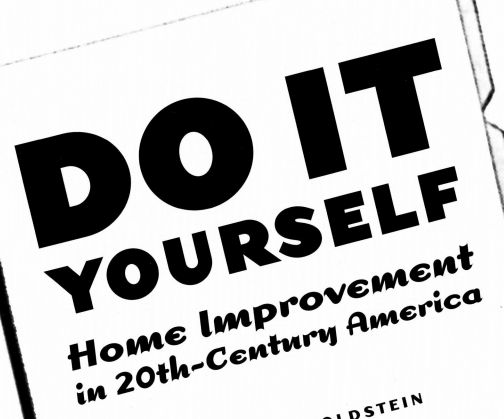

DO IT
YOURSELF

Home Improvement
in 20th-Century America

CAROLYN M. GOLDSTEIN

National Building Museum, Washington, D.C.

Princeton Architectural Press, New York

Do It Yourself:
Home Improvement in 20th-Century America
was made possible by a generous grant from the
American Hardware Manufacturers Association,
a national trade group representing 1,100 hardware
and home-improvement product makers.

Do It Yourself

Home Improvement in 20th-Century America